MOTIVATING
— YOUR —
CHURCH

MOTIVATING YOUR CHURCH

HOW *ANY* LEADER CAN IGNITE INTRINSIC MOTIVATION AND GROWTH

Dr. Paul P. Baard
Rev. Chris Aridas

A *Crossroad* Book
The Crossroad Publishing Company
New York

The Crossroad Publishing Company
481 Eighth Avenue, New York, NY 10001

Copyright © 2001 by Paul P. Baard and Chris Aridas

All rights reserved. No part of this book may be reproduced, stored in a retrieval system, or transmitted, in any form or by any means, electronic, mechanical, photocopying, recording, or otherwise, without the written permission of The Crossroad Publishing Company.

Printed in the United States of America

Scripture quotations are from the New American Bible with Revised New Testament (NAB), copyright © 1986 Confraternity of Christian Doctrine; and from the Holy Bible, New International Version (NIV), copyright © 1973, 1978, 1984 International Bible Society, and used by permission of Zondervan Publishing House.

Library of Congress Cataloging-in-Publication Data
Baard, Paul P.
   Motivating your church : how any leader can ignite intrinsic motivation and growth / by Paul P. Baard and Chris Aridas.
     p. cm.
   Includes bibliographical references.
   ISBN 0-8245-1894-2 (alk. paper)
   1. Church growth. I. Aridas, Chris, 1947- II. Title.
BV652.25 .B23 2001
254'.5–dc21
                                              2001001037

1   2   3   4   5   6   7   8   9   10   06   05   04   03   02   01

*To my daughter, Samantha,
and my wife, Veronica,
who are daily reminders
of God's love.*
– PAUL P. BAARD

*To my family of faith,
St. Margaret of Scotland Parish,
who continually manifest to me
the power of the Spirit.*
– FR. CHRIS ARIDAS

Contents

Preface	9
Acknowledgments	11
Introduction	15
1. Motivation: Why We Do and Why We Don't Do	21
2. Intrinsic Motivation: What Conditions Set Off This Wonderful Energy?	29
3. The Need for Competence	35
4. The Need for Relatedness	52
5. The Need for Autonomy	68
6. Developing Motivated Employees	84
7. Psychological Fusion: When Other People Can "Make Us Feel"	101
8. The Power of the Spirit	118
Appendix 1: Ministry Position Description	123
Appendix 2: Letter of Call	125
Appendix 3: Performance Appraisal Guidelines	127
Appendix 4: Church Motivation Assessment Tool	129
References	141

Preface

There are many fine leadership books devoted to church growth. Some explain the success of a particular congregation; others identify and organize the things vibrant churches do.

This book has as its focus the *people* behind it all. More specifically, it is about their energy—their motivation. You can find this variable between plans and programs:

Ideas → Motivation → Implementation.

The information you will encounter comes from a leading theory of motivation today, and is made practical by two men who have insights and experiences to share. Though we are from distinct branches of Christianity—an evangelical Protestant and a Roman Catholic—He who unites us is greater than any theological differences we have.

Acknowledgments

Writing a book is seldom an easy task. The challenge intensifies, however, when two people strive to produce a manuscript which remains faithful to the authors' different styles, thought processes, and religious experiences. Throw into that mix the unusual scenario of a New York-based author, juggling a full family life, academic career, and church responsibilities, with an active pastor taking a three-month sabbatical at a Trappist monastery where silence is the norm, and you have a most intriguing work situation! Several people, however, helped us accomplish the task at hand:

Colleagues Dr. Edward L. Deci and Dr. Richard M. Ryan, who valued and encouraged this application of their theory to church life; Rev. Joseph A. O'Hare, S.J., president of Fordham University, an early supporter of this work; Dr. Patrick J. Carroll, a mentor who taught me Bowen Systems Theory; Rev. F. Bryan Wilkerson, my pastor for many years; Samantha K. Baard, my intrinsically motivated daughter, inspiration, and assistant with some of the field research; Veronica K. Baard, my wife, friend, and partner; and Jesus Christ, my Savior and Lord, "through [whom] all things were made" (John 1:3 NIV).

—Dr. Paul P. Baard

Dennis Laderwager, pastoral associate, co-worker, and friend, who ably directed the parish's progress while I was away on sabbatical; the Trappist community at St. Joseph's Abbey,

Spencer, Massachusetts, who allowed me the unique privilege of participating fully in their life during my three-month sabbatical; Fr. Gerald Sears, O.C.S.O., who somehow rigged up a wireless Internet access in my monk's cell while I was at the monastery (the times surely are a changin'), thus allowing me to work long-distance with my co-author; and my good friend and mentor, Robert T. Heller, who continually provides ways for me to share my experience of ministry with others.

— REV. CHRIS ARIDAS

To all the above, we offer special thanks.

MOTIVATING
— YOUR —
CHURCH

Introduction

Each week in America more than 50 churches close their doors—permanently. (Barna 2000a)

In a public poll, 87 percent responded that the number one need in a pastor is the ability to motivate people to get involved. (Barna 2000c)

Who Needs a Church?

If you are involved in church ministry, you don't need us to acquaint you with the difficulties confronting organized religion today. While an overwhelming percentage of Americans claim to be believers in God, increasingly both pastors and pollsters hear: "Yes, I believe in God, but I can deal with him in my backyard. I don't need any church" (see Cimino and Lattin 1998; Gallup and Jones 2000).

Readers of this book know better. God wants us gathering with other believers (Heb. 10:25), and we need one another to stay on track (Prov. 27:17). Besides, a lack of participation in a local church has been linked with a distancing from God. Furthermore, if churches and denominations continue to weaken, who will fulfill the Great Commission: sending out missionaries to those in the greatest need around the world?

The number of men and women going into full-time ministry also remains at a relatively low level; a long-term crisis could be in the making. Even donations to churches, despite a vibrant economy for more than a decade, are depressed compared to only a generation ago (Ronsvalle and Ronsvalle 1998).

What accounts for this disengagement of Americans from their houses of worship? Many suggest it is the incredible level of busyness in our culture: fifty-, even sixty-hour workweeks, the extended school-day involvement of our kids, and so many competing "leisure time" activities. Others claim it is the secularization of society and the lack of family support systems that carried people in years past. We submit, however, the problem is a matter of motivation, or the lack of it, with respect to church. Even when there is a motivation to attend, give, or volunteer, too often it is not the best kind of drive. Some seem to act more out of a compulsion than an attraction, and this often leads to "burnout." While the next chapter examines the types of motivation more closely, a quick look ahead helps put the current challenge in a motivational perspective.

Motivation Energizes Behavior

Motivation explains why we do some things and do not do others. This book is devoted to exploring the kinds of motivation associated with church participation and ways to bring about the very best internal drive regarding church and a relationship with God. We will examine the psychological dynamics associated with "Christmas and Easter" Christians, and also look at the compulsively compliant—those who participate "religiously." Finally, we will investigate the conditions under which intrinsic motivation flourishes—the "I love being here, doing this!" type. Those church members you see with smiles on their faces as they cheerfully give of their talent and treasure are operating under this internal influence. All our research points to intrinsic motivation as the variable that accounts for church growth, increased attendance, and higher contribution and volunteerism levels. Make no mistake: we readily acknowledge that the Holy Spirit is the One who makes good things happen in a Christian church. Motivation simply appears to be the energizing force created within us into which the Spirit taps.

In the Church Engagement Model shown in chapter 1, we trace motivational inclinations over the life-span of a maturing individual. The initial awe and wonder children have for our Creator God is typically left behind in adolescence, ironically at a time when many Christian churches celebrate Confirmation, often taken as a public declaration that "this is now *my* religion." While some teenagers remain active in a church because of genuine, personal love for God and his people, too many seem to be there merely to comply with their parents' wishes. Still more simply walk away from church, even from God. Church leaders then observe many coming back when they have their own children in order to be "good parents." But after their kids go off to college, there is another drop off. Finally, some return in their later years to "fix things up" for the hereafter. In the chapters to follow, we will examine these underlying motivational processes and make some suggestions for ways to use this knowledge strategically.

Motivation Explains Church Growth

At the outset, we acknowledge that these are not necessarily the best times to run a church (although an argument could be made that this is a far better atmosphere than when Christianity first began!). Some sociologists suggest there is a negative correlation between the strength of an economy and the level of church participation of its citizens. Still other academics and church researchers say there are trends in the types of churches that do well. Those denominations that have the "in" style, for example, flourish for a time. Today evangelical

Protestant churches are considered "in," and mainline Protestant churches "out." Roman Catholic churches are reported to be essentially flat, with Catholic losses in North America offset by the influx of Catholic immigrants, particularly from Central and South America.

Yet these sociological trends do not explain the experiences of some individual churches. When measured by attendance, contributions, and individuals who are growing in their relationship with the Lord, some of the greatest successes in recent years have been in mainline Protestant and Roman Catholic churches. And, while evangelical Protestantism is growing, many of its churches close their doors each week. What's *really* going on? We submit it is a matter of leadership, and we don't mean the presence of a charismatic dynamo. Smartly run churches offer the same wonderful message: God offers everyone his love, forgiveness, and grace. Making God's message and the church boring and irrelevant—two top complaints of former churchgoers—is inexcusable.

Motivation: The Critical Ingredient

First we will take a look at this critical ingredient in churchgoing: motivation. Then we will share with you what is arguably the leading theory of motivation in the world today, colleagues Edward Deci (pronounced DEE-see) and Richard Ryan's theory of intrinsic motivation. Subsequent chapters will provide ideas on how to bring about the very best motivation and avoid accidentally crushing it out. Because most church leaders also have an interest in motivating employees, we include this topic as well.

Many of us have to deal at times with people who seem "amotivated" (apparently lacking any purposeful intent), whether due to burnout or some other variable. Borrowing heavily from the work done in the psychological field of behaviorism, we devote a chapter to addressing "problem employees," or, better said, employees with a problem. You will be encouraged to see how motivation can be reignited in these people.

Appendix 1 is a sample Ministry Position Description, and appendix 2 a sample letter of call. Appendix 3 provides performance appraisal guidelines, and appendix 4 offers an instrument to help church leaders assess their church's motivation atmosphere.

•

By now, a few thoughts may have crossed your mind:

1. This stuff seems pretty obvious.

We agree: "There is nothing new under the sun" (Eccles. 1:9 NIV). However, as you will see, some of the assertions in this book—backed by good research and practice—are counterintuitive. After all, one of the best-selling management books of the 1990s was *Punished by Rewards* (Kohn 1993). Punished—rewards? Sure, if they are used in a manipulative manner, as they often are. At the minimum, we believe you will recognize those experiences that left you really excited about the work or study you do. And you'll be able to label, and avoid doing, the things that did not work out well.

2. Who has time to do these things?

We submit that any church leader who has the time to worry about declining attendance and giving and strains to find volunteers to perform the many tasks associated with running a church has the time to implement these suggestions. Just picture the delight you will take in seeing more smiling faces on a Sunday morning and in having plentiful resources with which to do so much more of God's work! The investment you make in studying this book and implementing its findings should prove to be a very strategic one.

3. Are we talking about major changes?

Many church leadership books call for a virtual reinvention of a congregation. This often creates emotional strain, and sometimes financial drain, as leaders try to implement changes. Worse still, congregations can become divided, especially if the top leadership does not endorse the changes.

We have found in our research and seminars, however, that *one person* can make a difference in the motivational lives of those in his or her circle of influence—a difference that does not require elaborate structural changes, complicated plans, or unlimited financial resources. *By attending to what and how a leader says and does things, intrinsic motivation can be ignited.* Just by becoming aware of these principles of motivation, you can easily tweak your style to accommodate them. Our hope is that in the course of reading this book, church leaders will experience an insight that enables them to understand and embrace a leadership style that releases the reservoir of intrinsic motivation within their congregations.

Hang on for a journey into the minds and motivations of your flock, therefore, as we delve into the world of intrinsic motivation and explore ideas that you can implement in everyday exchanges with your congregation, employees, and volunteers.

And while our focus is motivation, the final chapter is devoted to God, and God alone. Without him, through the working of his Spirit, our efforts to reach and nurture individuals for Christ will be in vain (Ps. 127:1). Yet with God, *everything* is possible (Matt. 19:26).

Chapter One

Motivation

Why We Do and Why We Don't Do

Person A: I go to church because I feel especially close to God in worship. I enjoy being with his people, and I love to learn more about him.

*Person B: I go to church because people **should** go (and I want to balance the score with the wrong things that I do).*

Person C: I hardly ever go to church; it's not really relevant to my busy life. Besides, all they really want is my money, and I don't know many people there.

Motivation is about *why* we do some things and don't do other things. The above comments reflect different types of motivation people experience regarding church. You will see that there are three basic kinds of motivation we all encounter in our daily lives, whether at home, church, work, or play.

Intrinsic Motivation

Person "A" above is moved by what is called *intrinsic motivation:* "I really want to be here, doing this." The experience of this kind of drive is familiar to those who enjoy a hobby or sport. Count yourself particularly blessed if this is how your job feels much of the time, or at least when you begin a special, challenging assignment or undertake a new initiative. The feeling is one of enjoyment, even excitement. The activity is engaging, providing "stretch" to current abilities or knowledge. There is no pressure associated with these tasks, except maybe that which we put upon ourselves to reach a new level of skill or understanding. There's a marvelous sense of freedom since we have chosen to be there, doing that activity. Nobody cajoled or pressured us into our involvement.

This very natural drive—intrinsic motivation—"is an inherent tendency to seek out novel challenges, to extend one's capacities, to explore, and to learn," according to leading motivational theorists Edward Deci and Richard Ryan, whose theory drives this book (Ryan and Deci 2000; Deci 1995). With intrinsic motivation, we seek out challenges to our current knowledge or ability. We enjoy playing an opponent slightly better than ourselves. We take on a new task at the job or at church and feel the growth in our capacities. Mind you, it does not mean an unreasonable challenge, which some leaders are bent on inflicting on those under them. "Even though we have three fewer tellers, let's make sure the customers of this bank experience the same high level of service as before!" the clueless, Dilbert-described boss intones after a layoff.

Intrinsic motivation is that rich drive which accompanies engagement in an activity for no reason other than the innate satisfaction it provides. No external inducements are needed: we just want to do it, to be there. This natural drive can lead to working on a crossword puzzle, playing tennis, or going to church to learn more about God and his ways. No pressure, just enjoyment. You can probably recall a particular church event—perhaps a joyous wedding celebration or a poignant funeral service—which left you feeling especially grateful for having been there. Ideally, this motivational state is a regular occurrence for you at your church. But for far too many, it is either rare or a nonoccurrence.

We'll have more to say about intrinsic motivation, and how it comes to be, in the next chapter.

Extrinsic Motivation

Person "B" above is describing the experience of *extrinsic motivation,* that is, engaging in something in order to get a reward or to avoid a punishment. When we compete to win a tennis tournament prize or strain to complete a work or school assignment by its due date, we are in an extrinsic motivational state. Similarly, it is extrinsic motivation that accounts for going to church to avoid feelings of guilt or doing so to earn some nonintrinsic outcome (everything from the admiration of our neighbors to, as some believe, improving their odds for getting to heaven).

Extrinsic motivation involves a focus on an outcome separate from the activity itself. It isn't simply delighting in the matter at hand, but rather in some extra benefit one might derive from it. This type of drive is usually accompanied by the experience of pressure and stress. For example, most children begin playing a sport because of the satisfaction inherent in hitting a ball or getting a shot into the net. Somewhere along the line for too many of them, getting a trophy for hitting, scoring, or team rank becomes the only satisfaction of the sport. Pressure to win replaces the thrill of a challenge to one's current ability level. Cheating becomes a little more palatable. In one community, the first question raised by potential participants in a new baseball league being formed was "How big will the trophies be?"

In his leadership best-seller, *Punished by Rewards,* Alfie Kohn documents many research studies that reveal the deleterious effects of introducing extrinsic rewards to what had been an intrinsically rewarding activity. And the process is often insidious. A child discovers the joy of playing the piano. She takes lessons and has the fun of performing richer, more challenging pieces of music. Her instructor suggests she enter a statewide competition; she does so and does well. Now her parents' car is emblazoned with a bumper-sticker telling the world they are the proud parents of a state finalist. The child has gone from the pure joy of music to a very cheapened experience of playing to get a plastic trophy and to earn bragging rights for her parents. It won't be long, the research tells us, before she stops playing entirely.

A number of experiments conducted some time ago shed light on the matter of introducing extrinsic rewards to what had been an intrinsically motivated activity. One prototype was carried out by Edward L. Deci (Deci 1971). In his experiment, he divided college students into two groups, one a control group and the other an experimental one. The task assigned was the solution of a mechanical spatial-relations puzzle called Soma. This puzzle involved differently shaped pieces that could be arranged into varying configurations. The task given to the students was to match a picture with the materials provided. (Early trials had revealed these Soma puzzles were intrinsically interesting to the college student population.) In the first session, both groups merely worked on four puzzles each over a thirteen-minute time period. During the second session, however, the control group was informed that each member would receive a one dollar reward for each puzzle solved (considered an acceptable incentive at the time). By then creating "free period" opportunities (several were made available) for students in both the control and experimental conditions, the experimenter was able to assess the level of intrinsic motivation remaining toward the puzzles in each group. As predicted, those who received an extrinsic reward for completion of the puzzles chose to do fewer puzzles during the free period than those who did not have such incentives attached to that activity. What had been an intrinsically rewarding activity had been undermined by extrinsic rewards. "What's in it for me?" replaced "This is interesting!"

Extrinsic motivation also comes about when a church relies on cajoling people to volunteer: "Please, do this as a personal favor for me," intones the pastor. It happens too when giving at a certain level gets a member onto the "Bishop's List" for a celebratory banquet. Or when a Las Vegas Night is used to seduce those who enjoy the chance to hit the jackpot. Make no mistake, each of these devices may work in the short term, but none earns a true commitment for the long haul.

A harried pastor reading this chapter might think, "Hey, I'll take extrinsic motivation: at least they are showing up, giving, and volunteering! Call it what you will—things get done."

Regrettably, while it is true that extrinsic motivation does correlate with better attendance, giving, and volunteering than does amotivation, extrinsic motivation often *leads* to amotivation. Extrinsic incentives are not benign: "If they don't want the incentive, they can pass on it!" Such tactics have been found to turn people off, and away. Using extrinsic incentives to entice participation is *manipulation,* not motivation.

Amotivation

Person "C" described above is suffering from amotivation, or nonpurposefulness regarding church involvement. Amotivation often comes about when an individual senses that an activity is either impossible to accomplish or has no personally meaningful consequence even if it were performed. Examples of this regrettable state include doing the bare minimum in order to get through a class or simply not participating in an event because one expects to fail. It's about not going to church because it appears irrelevant to one's daily concerns, or because it seems impossible to meet perceived expectations there. Almost anything else is "more important." Amotivation also comes about when people feel used, manipulated, or disregarded.

When we observe the lifecycle of churchgoers, a disturbing pattern is all too familiar to seasoned church leaders. Figure 1 on the following page illustrates the Church Engagement Model. Most start out in church having an intrinsically motivating experience. The toddler feels the warmth of teachers sharing the fact that our great God made all things and loves us dearly (see Cavalletti 1983 for groundbreaking work indicating a child's openness to God). But over time, things change for many of our young ones. The lessons become redundant, and the answers to questions more platitudinal, even in church schools. Somehow "cool" with friends doesn't seem to include loving God, thanks perhaps to hostile attitudes in the media and public school systems. Adolescence brings competing demands on time as well as encounters with alternative philosophies and the questioning of such things as moral absolutes. Then it's off to college and a world of almost unlimited non-Christian choices. Experience has shown that some of these individuals return when they have their own children. After all, they want to be "good parents" (an extrinsic motivation) who dedicate or baptize their children and provide for Sunday school experiences. When their offspring hit the teen years, however, many simply return to the golf course or shopping mall on Sunday mornings. One final influx occurs: in later years, many are either lonely or are taking no chances, fearing a Day of Judgment (again an extrinsic motivation).

Effective church leaders are using this knowledge to "offer motivational opportunities." For example, since many new

Figure 1. Church Engagement Model by Paul P. Baard, Ph.D.

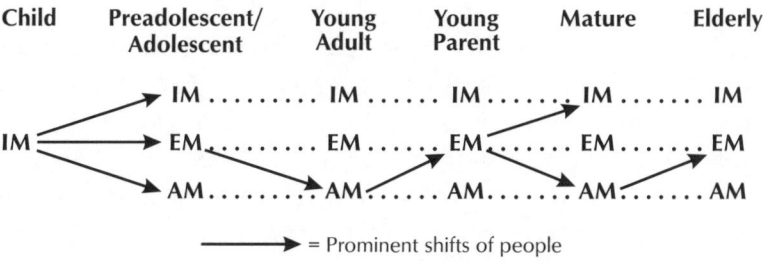

———▶ = Prominent shifts of people

IM = **Intrinsic Motivation:** delighting in an activity or relationship; experiencing choice, challenge, and connectedness

EM = **Extrinsic Motivation:** participating mostly because of incentive or fear of ill consequences; sense of pressure

AM = **Amotivation:** barely involved or eventually dropping out; feeling task is impossible or irrelevant

---

parents seek the help of the church to instruct their little ones in the basics of the faith, why not present a compelling topic for Mom and Dad at the same time so they willingly park the car and stay the hour? And years later, after the nest empties out, why not keep these people hooked in by scheduling activities that truly meet their motivational needs as middle-age or senior citizens? We'll spell out some particulars in the upcoming chapters.

We are setting out to find ways for us to tap into the richest kind of motivation—intrinsic motivation. The case for pursuing intrinsic motivation is compelling. It is not coincidental that intrinsically motivated activity results in greater productivity and lower stress. A large body of research shows that when people are operating out of this drive, they are more committed, creative, and productive, and a whole lot happier about the place they are in (Deci and Ryan 1985). The studies have been conducted in school, at work, at home, in sports arenas, and in church settings. The more intrinsic motivation, the greater one's commitment.

Besides, as a simple matter of survival, the church and its leaders need to focus on intrinsic motivation because we are *dependent* upon it. People no longer feel they *have* to come to church. The church needs to create an environment in which people *want* to participate. And our employees had better be getting something very special out of their work at church; we can't afford to compete on an extrinsic basis—one of pay and promotional opportunities.

So let's look at what it takes to present an intrinsically motivating environment. We take great comfort in noting the clear biblical support for the theory's assertions and begin "need" chapters with relevant illustrative passages from Scripture.

Chapter Two

Intrinsic Motivation

What Conditions Set Off This Wonderful Energy?

The two sixty-year-old men lunge and run in their hotly contested handball game. When asked who usually wins, they respond: "Wins? We don't keep score. We're having too much fun!"

Intrinsic motivation: doing something for the pure joy inherent in the task. It's there at birth. Watch the newborn explore her world. The child gazes out from her crib and is obviously eager to learn, first putting objects in her mouth, then crawling to new places, and on she goes. And why does a young boy so resist being cajoled into doing something that his parents want done but that isn't very interesting to him? Finally, what accounts for a child's great desire to be accepted by family and friends? Each of these observable behaviors reflects *intrinsic motivation,* which accounts for the very best energy evident in human beings. It is the motivation that leads us to explore, to be free, to connect with others—well before we learn the business about earning grades, admiration, and approval. Each of these aforementioned behaviors finds its energy innately within.

We experience intrinsic motivation in many ways in our daily lives, and when we allow this natural energy to direct our actions, invigorating things happen. For example, the book read because of a compelling interest in the topic or author is far more satisfying than the book read because it is on a student's required reading list. The tennis match against a good buddy is inherently more satisfying than the one played to win in organized competition. A host of academic and applied field research studies have affirmed these conclusions (Deci and Ryan 1985). Students do better at school work, athletes perform at a higher level, those in creative roles excel in their art, and workers achieve greater productivity (while experiencing less stress) when these activities are energized by intrinsic motivation.

And for churches, intrinsic motivation has been linked with

- more frequent attendance
- higher levels of donations of time and money, and
- better internalization of Christian values.

While *extrinsic motivation*—the striving, often compulsive kind—does get people to show up, give, and volunteer, it has been found to lead to burnout and dropout, which psychologists call *amotivation*.

Research of Deci and Ryan

So what experiences account for the profound differences in the way people approach church? Think of the "Christmas and Easter" Christians. Was it their upbringing? a bad encounter with clergy? shame for a sinful life? Is there a downside to those who seem neurotically drawn to church, often engaged in compulsive rituals? And how is it that other people utterly delight in being in God's house and with his people? Is it the presence of a charismatic pastor? Most importantly, how can we, as leaders, bring about this richer motivational atmosphere in more churches, including those without "superstars" at the helm?

Researchers Edward Deci and Richard Ryan of the University of Rochester in New York have developed, arguably, the leading theory of motivation in the world today. Their Cognitive Evaluation Theory articulates the conditions under which intrinsic motivation thrives. These academic psychologists and their colleagues have conducted elaborate research identifying three innate psychological needs with which human beings are endowed. Not surprising to the readers of this book, we suppose, is the fact that each of these needs can be readily identified in the very first chapters of Genesis. When these psychological needs, often more powerful than physiological needs, are satisfied, that wonderful state of intrinsic motivation occurs. When they are frustrated, people eventually become amotivated.

When church members were asked to evaluate how well these needs were being met in their church experience (see appendix 4 for a description of the research methodology), higher satisfaction of the aforementioned needs was associated with growth in membership, attendance, and contribution levels, and the spiritual vitality of the churches' attendees.

Motivational Needs and Intrinsic Motivation

While each of these motivational needs is described in greater detail in separate chapters to follow, here is a preview:

1. The Need for Competence

The need for competence involves experiencing an optimal challenge to our current knowledge or abilities. It is learning and putting our skills to work—stretching beyond our comfort level. We like to play someone slightly better than ourselves in our favorite sport. A feeling of growth is the result of satisfying the need for competence. A litmus test to see if this development is taking place in your church is to ask church members: "Do you know God better than you did a year ago?"

Engaging sermons, insightful teaching, and small group discussions all permit this need for competence to be satisfied. Platitudinal sermons or homilies and clichés served up when a person is hurting serve to frustrate this need.

2. The Need for Relatedness

The need for relatedness pertains to being in a mutually reliant relationship. It's about feeling loved and accepted for who one truly is; it includes caring for others and being cared for by others. This is the innate need that explains altruistic behavior. It is behind our very natural inclination to be in supportive relationships with neighbors and friends, extending to the most intimate human relationship—marriage.

This need for relatedness can be well satisfied in a family of believers, yet it is here—at church—where the need for connecting is so often frustrated. Cliques—those groups that tend toward exclusion of newcomers and others not considered sufficiently desirable—are conspicuous violations of this need of inclusion.

In a subsequent chapter, we will take a closer look at this need and present ideas on how to satisfy it in your church. We will also offer cautions about how this need is sometimes frustrated by well-intentioned leaders and provide suggestions for how to ameliorate these limitations. Since the same intrinsic motivation that propels attendance, giving, and serving at church also affects effectiveness at work and a myriad of other involvements, some tips on motivating employees are included in the following chapters.

3. The Need for Autonomy

There is something distinctly enjoyable about being in a situation because we genuinely choose to be there or to give of self or money because of a belief in a cause. This contrasts vividly to those times we feel caught up in something we were talked into. The former is exciting; the latter is stressful, often leaving us resentful of leaders—even ourselves—for agreeing to do whatever we were asked. The variable is the level of self-determination or autonomy we sense. Please note, autonomy is *not* about self-centeredness, but rather self-choice.

Regrettably, in their enthusiasm to accomplish a task in a church, leaders sometimes violate the need for autonomy as they try to persuade reluctant volunteers to take on a ministry. Sometimes this is done overtly: "C'mon, Tom, I really need you on this." Other times the approach is more subtle: "Sue, this is your call. I'm just in a bind right now, and I would consider this a personal favor."

Either of these approaches compromises the need for autonomy in the would-be volunteer, and ultimately the impact on motivation will likely be disastrous. Oh, yes, that person probably will meet the commitment. But in the long term, he or she will move away from the perceived source of pressure—from the pastor, the lay leader, the church, and possibly even God.

The research paradigm used for many of the studies referred to here is depicted in figure 2 on the following page.

Among the important findings related to Deci and Ryan's theory of intrinsic motivation is that satisfaction of innate motivational needs is not an all-or-nothing arrangement. If you are not a perfect leader, therefore, you can still expect to see high levels of intrinsic motivation in followers. The research suggests that it will be to the *degree* that these needs are met that the fruits of intrinsically motivated participation will appear.

Figure 2. Motivation Research Model:
Outcomes Associated with Intrinsic Need Satisfaction

Needs	Outcomes
• Competence	• Attending
• Relatedness	• Giving
• Autonomy	• Volunteering
	• Entering Full-Time Ministry*

*This correlation is hypothesized based on research linking intrinsic need satisfaction with higher levels of integration of Christian values; a research plan for empirical investigation of this relationship is in development.

So the better you get at challenging your people while assuring their ability to meet those challenges, the more they feel a mutual reliance between you and them, and the greater their sense of influencing how things get done in the church, the more intrinsically motivated they will be. And the more intrinsically motivated they are, the more growth your church can anticipate.

We now turn to some specific suggestions you can implement in the daily life of your church.

Chapter Three

The Need for Competence

Have dominion over... all the living things that move on the earth"
—Genesis 1:28b NAB

People want to feel they are part of something big and meaningful, that their lives are making a difference and their involvement with various causes is having an impact on others. It's why a leader's vision is so important. For example, Martin Luther King Jr. had a dream that mobilized not only people of color, but all who could see a better America in which "the sons of former slaves and the sons of former slave owners will be able to sit down together at the table of brotherhood." Mother Teresa saw the dignity of the poorest of the poor, and so they felt the love of Christ in their final days on earth instead of dying in squalor and abandonment. Walt Disney envisioned a magnificent place of family entertainment and "saw" Disney World in Florida, even though he did not live to see its opening day.

Jesus shared his vision with us when he said, "Therefore go and make disciples of all nations" (Matt. 28:19 NIV). This objective shows up locally: "I see our church changing many individual lives, even our whole community!" as one pastor declared in kicking off a building expansion at a small suburban church. Every member of the congregation donated to that drive. Contributions far exceeded expectations as those with lesser means gave of their limited savings while others forsook remodeling their homes in order to "provide a seat in which someone might come to meet Christ" (from the campaign's brochure). There was a passion for the vision, on the part of both leaders and followers. All felt they were a part of a worthy mission. Today that church serves three times as many people as it did just five years ago. The pastor and leadership had tapped into the intrinsic motivation of the members.

Leaders have many opportunities in the day-to-day life of their churches to help people experience the excitement of being part of something of consequence. In particular, the ministries of a church provide many occasions in which members can satisfy their need for competence—to grow, to make a difference by serving, by learning, and by teaching.

The Theory

Theorists Deci and Ryan define the need for competence as the need to master our environment, to have an impact, and to stretch our knowledge and abilities. This drive is innate, not learned. We can observe an infant straining to lift her head to see what's outside her crib. Soon she will be standing to get a better look and then trying to get out on the floor to crawl, to walk, and then to run to new destinations—all in a quest to know her world. And she won't be doing it to win a prize or a parent's approval. The need for competence is an inborn source of energy, and her satisfaction comes from the process itself—growing in knowledge and ability.

The need for competence also involves feeling effective in an endeavor. It doesn't simply mean "I am capable of a task," but rather "Through this task I can accomplish a goal I have." For example, while most students can do high school level work, some fail at it because they do not see how earning a degree helps them achieve their career goals. The competence drive is a particularly persistent one, explaining why we often endure in our attempts at difficult tasks. This energy to learn, master, increase in knowledge, use our skills and abilities, shows up in many domains. We enjoy opportunities to do different things on the job. We read "How to" books (even this one!), take courses, pay for lessons, all in a quest for mastery.

A key variable associated with the competence drive is the notion of "optimal challenge." Too much challenge leads to failure and amotivation (try stepping onto a court with a tennis pro), while too little stretch leads to boredom and amotivation (the same court, only now with a beginner). We want to be challenged, to keep learning and growing all through our lives.

The need for competence, then, is about experiencing growth and using one's abilities. In the church realm it is drawing closer to God each year, knowing God's ways, and serving him in a meaningful manner. We can feel this need being satisfied when we help solve a problem at church (mastering our environment), make a sacrificial gift to a cause (having an impact), or leave a worship service knowing something more than when we went in (stretching our knowledge and abilities).

This chapter focuses on that innate, psychological need for competence, arguably the most important need to be met in order for church members to have an intrinsically motivated experience. We now look at some opportunities our congregations have to meet this need, and what we sometimes inadvertently do to frustrate it.

"Am I Growing Spiritually?" and "Do I Know God Now Better Than a Year Ago?"

These questions serve as a rough self-assessment (a more refined empirical measure appears in appendix 4). While churches meet many human needs, spiritual vitality is, of course, their raison d'être. In our churches, we are either "growing or going" (that is, leaving), our research suggests. God has clearly designed us to work, to learn, to get things done. God gave us the Scriptures (written in the everyday language used at the time of their writing) so all could learn of him and his ways. Jesus came to teach us about the Father, as well as to save us from our sins—a task impossible for us on our own. The Holy Spirit was sent to help us to better understand the Scriptures and to grow in our relationship with Jesus. And, although he did not need us, God included us in his work with that Great Commission to make disciples of all. Each of these matters points to our innate drive for competence in the spiritual domain: to grow in holiness, to have an impact, to serve God and his people.

Being drawn to opportunities for spiritual maturation, therefore, is crucial to one's initial interest in a church community, as well as one's decision to belong to a particular church. Some have declared to us: "Churches shouldn't have to make their offerings motivational. People should go to their own church because, well, they *should!*" The simple reality is that if people only hear the painfully obvious ("Do good and avoid evil") or if they must endure the unfathomable and esoteric ("What is he talking about?"), they will be disinclined to return to the place that psychologically disengaged them. Intrinsic motivation is about *optimal* challenge to current knowledge and abilities; without this, we either become extrinsically motivated (trying to "earn points" to avoid hell or attempting to get a prayer answered), or amotivated ("this just isn't for me").

Just as minimally engaging messages fail to satisfy the need for competence, suboptimal challenges to our abilities produce the same results: "Will you teach the fourth-graders again? I know this would be your thirteenth year, but we really need...?" Not much opportunity for growth here, unless the teacher is encouraged to try out a new curriculum. And just as very difficult sermons and homilies (whether esoteric in content or merciless in their admonitions) disengage listeners, so do maximal challenges for the work to be done: "I know it may be tough for someone in their eighties to take on the responsibility for our teen program, but we need coverage." Assignments that could appear daunting ("We've got to come up with one million dollars for our building campaign!") must be accompanied with credible assurance of support of their efforts if volunteers are to meet the litmus test of being challenged optimally. The task must be perceived as doable, albeit with a bit of stretch.

Competence at Church: Supports and Frustrations

What follows is a "starter list" of possible ways church leaders can meet the need for competence in their churches. (We will offer such a list at the end of each "need" chapter.) Our purpose is not to provide an all-inclusive program for you to implement. It's simply to encourage you to imagine anew some ways that the need for competence might be fulfilled in your particular situation. In presenting this list, we do wish to acknowledge, however, that the sermon or homily is the single, greatest opportunity to satisfy the need of members and visitors to grow. For that reason we place this crucial matter at the top of our list.

1. Deliver Engaging Sermons or Homilies*

Whether your church is in the Catholic or Protestant tradition, your attendance and membership levels very likely corre-

---

*There is a difference between a sermon and a homily as understood in different Christian churches. Among Protestant churches, the sermon is often a central focus

late significantly with the perceived quality of the preaching and teaching that takes place. At one time, this statement would be true primarily of Protestant houses of worship, as the sacraments pretty much carried the day in Roman Catholic churches. This is no longer the case. Roman Catholic priest and author Andrew Greeley observes that the strength of sermons has become a major factor in where Catholics choose to worship (Greeley 1984). According to one study of church participation, of the three components of intrinsic motivation—the needs for competence, relatedness, and autonomy—competence was found to be the greatest variable in whether a church was growing or declining in membership, attendance, and giving levels (Baard 1994a). And of the identified components contributing to competence, quality of the sermon or homily was the greatest. There is no getting away from this fact: America has become a place of church-shopping, both within and across denominations (Cimino and Lattin 1998). In the past decade, even Roman Catholics have parted from tradition, no longer hesitating to move across parish or denominational lines in order to experience the sense of spiritual nourishment and growth they receive from the sermon or homily.

Whether you are a minister or priest or serve in another leadership role, this first topic is vital for you to address. Even if you are not the preacher, you are in a position to influence or perhaps encourage or support the preacher in that endeavor. If the message is not of high caliber, your increas-

---

in the worship service. For that reason the length of a sermon can be substantial as the preacher develops a particular theme based on a Scripture text, often using additional passages for amplification. It is not unusual for the sermon to have a title indicating the theme and content. In the Roman Catholic tradition, the homily draws on the Scripture readings of the day, with the intention of explaining the faith and the standards of the Christian life, taking into account the needs of listeners. Because a Sunday homily is part of a liturgical service, it necessarily has certain time constraints and must be integrated into the experience of the Eucharist of which it is a part.

ingly sophisticated members, better educated than they were a generation ago, are now more able to discern the effort the preacher puts into the sermon.

Sermon length is an interesting variable. Recent research by a communications scholar (Carrell 2000) revealed an unexpected finding: both Catholic and Protestant congregations reported the ideal sermon length to be *longer* than did their respective pastors. While Catholic priests thought the ideal to be nine minutes, their flock preferred fifteen. Similarly, Protestant preachers considered twenty-two minutes ideal, and those in the assembly wanted twenty-five. Since this survey included more than five hundred churchgoers and one hundred preachers nationwide, these differences are statistically significant. (Perhaps the heretofore unknown gap is explained by the fact that Carrell's research also revealed that 78 percent of churchgoers report they never offer their priests or preachers any feedback about the sermon.)

Again, the single greatest opportunity any congregation has to meet the innate motivational need to grow, to learn more, is through the weekly sermon or homily. So what priority do church leaders assign to this matter? Again we turn to Carrell's recent findings: Roman Catholic priests reported an average of three hours per week devoted to sermon preparation, while Protestant ministers reported eleven hours.

We realize that, for various reasons, homily preparation time often gets short shrift among Roman Catholic clergy. Most Roman Catholic congregations are substantially larger than Protestant ones, thereby increasing the demands of sacramental ministry. In addition, Roman Catholic congregations (and hierarchy) traditionally have expected their clergy to be always available, tending to every detail of parish life. Furthermore, only with the liturgical renewal brought about by the Second Vatican Council has the homily's importance been rediscovered within the Catholic community. For these reasons, homily preparation time often has been lost amid the other "priorities" placed upon the clergy. Nevertheless, the authors contend that by striving to fulfill the congregation's need for competence in this area, the members' expectations will begin to change (especially with regard to constant availability). This, in turn, will free the clergy to respond to Catholic critic Andrew Greeley's observations that priests must improve the quality of their message (Greeley 1984).

Carrell's research revealed that both Catholic and Protestant churchgoers employ the same criteria in judging quality, namely, insights gained, impact on their spiritual lives, and relevance to daily living. They disagree only about sermon length, perhaps because of learned expectations or the context in which the message appears, that is, as a relatively small part of the Roman Catholic eucharistic celebration but a dominant position in the worship service in most Protestant traditions.*

"But not everyone is equally gifted in this area!" you might rightly claim. While this is certainly a fact, even a church minister whose strength is not in preaching, with adequate effort in preparation can deliver a message which truly offers the type of spiritual nourishment people crave. There are numerous resource materials available: Bible commentaries such as those by F. F. Bruce and William Barclay and the Liturgical Press Collegeville Bible Commentary series, as well as a host of new Internet sites. Web pages such as *TextWeek.com, ForMinistry.com, homilies.com, opsouth.org,* and *equip.org* provide immediate retrieval of Scripture texts by topic and verse from all major translations of the Bible as well as contemporary renditions. Some of these online sites

---

*Some Catholic pastoral ministers argue that the schedule for their masses will not allow them to extend the homily. In view of the need for competence, however, one might want to consider changing the schedule of the masses so that there is more time between celebrations. This, of course, should be done in consultation with parish members (see chapter 5, "The Need for Autonomy").

have the liturgical calendar for major denominations, including Roman Catholic, and provide instant access to that week's readings along with commentary from noted scholars.

Simply put, the need for competence is satisfied when church members learn something new that is relevant to their walk with Christ. While this is most readily achieved in a weekly message, it can also be accomplished through other learning experiences such as those listed below.

2. Build Scripture Reflection and Faith-Sharing Experiences into Church Meetings

Individual Christians can experience a sense of nourishment and growth simply by sharing their faith with others. For that reason, whenever church members gather for a meeting, sharing God's Word through the reading of a Scripture text at the start of the gathering can become an ongoing source of strength for all who participate. In many churches, a typical meeting begins with a prayer, often perfunctory, asking God to bless whatever the leaders, in fact, already decided to do. Why not consider expanding that period of prayer to include the reading of God's Word, after which those present can spend a few moments sharing with one another how they have tried to incorporate the Word of God into their own lives. Here we offer a word of caution. Avoid the temptation of keeping a large group together when inviting members to share their responses. Far better to break into small groups of two or three, thereby allowing everyone the opportunity to share.

The amount of additional time this might add to a meeting is minimal: ten minutes at most, including the reading of the Scripture text. The payoff in the long run, however, is inestimable. As people *share* with others their victories and struggles and *learn* from the victories and struggles of others, they find themselves growing in faith, thus fulfilling the need for competence. Needless to say, one cannot be forced to enter into this experience. For that reason, dividing into groups of two or three allows people the freedom to "pass" without feeling undue pressure to say something. Experience has shown that even those who choose not to share something will still find their need for competence fulfilled as they learn from those who have chosen to share.

3. Provide Age- and Time-Appropriate Study Opportunities

Small group Bible study has been found extremely effective for evangelization. One Roman Catholic diocese began a program, Renew 2000, that tied into the Jubilee Year, equipping its parishes with appropriate teaching and discussion materials in order to engage those who had distanced themselves from church. In a matter of months, thousands who had stopped attending church—invited by caring neighbors—returned. An evangelical Protestant church, through a weekly daytime Bible study for women begun by the pastor's wife, had similar results. Through this process many people experienced, for the first time, the realization that God's teachings could be clarified and made relevant.

Accessible classes and study or discussion groups are increasing in popularity. These can be offered at different times for different groups: soccer moms (in the morning, after school begins), commuting dads (one church started a men's study on a morning train), local tradesmen (over coffee at a diner every Thursday at 7:00 A.M.). Each venue provides a chance to grapple with practical as well as theological issues. Adult, children, and student Sunday schools are options. One Roman Catholic parish conducted an adult learning hour from 11:30 A.M. to 12:30 P.M. (after one mass ended and before the next one began), open to anyone interested. The format was a brief presentation by a catechist, followed by small discussion groups. Tied into the parish's RCIA process,* the program enabled those preparing for entrance into the church to learn and share faith along with those who were already members of the community. For all involved, the experience proved edifying and supportive.

Just as specific days and times work for only a limited number of people, discussion topics sometimes have limited appeal. "Biblical Insights for Child-Rearing" will not necessarily draw the elderly or single person. It's best to poll your members regularly (perhaps with a bulletin insert) and, if feasible, present a series of lecture or study choices. If a church's educational resources are limited, for example, only a few members have a gift for teaching, consider a "buddy effort" with neighboring Christian congregations in your community. The appearance of a good lecturer on a relevant topic could unite fellow Christians, and any doctrinal differences might be addressed in subsequent meetings. This was accomplished quite successfully in the New York area some years ago during a Billy Graham Crusade. The Roman Catholic diocese on Long Island effectively mobilized many to attend this evangelical event, after which the diocese sponsored local Bible study groups for those Catholics who attended the rally.

4. Set Achievable Goals

While biblical mandates about holiness cannot be compromised, sometimes a sermon can be overwhelming, especially to someone new to the Christian faith. When preachers admit to their own struggles with a spiritual issue, however, listeners are better able to relate, realizing they are not the only ones finding it hard, at times, to live the Christian life.

---

*In the Roman Catholic tradition, those seeking entrance into the church participate in a formation process called the Rite of Christian Initiation of Adults, RCIA for short.

Similarly, when volunteers take on new tasks, church leaders need to provide support, including helping the volunteers to set realistic expectations for themselves. Frequently volunteers accept responsibility for a task without realizing all that is involved. It is important for leaders to invest time in volunteers, making sure that they remain realistic about what can be accomplished. Nothing undermines the need for competence more than setting up volunteers for failure. To avoid this, it might be helpful to use a "Ministry Position Description" that outlines what is expected, what gifts are needed to accomplish the task, the time commitment involved, and the support that will be provided. A sample description appears in appendix 1 (p. 123).

5. Foster Members' Talents

To use a God-given gift for the Lord's purposes is one of the most exciting things about being a Christian. Think of it: God willed this whole world into being. He certainly does not need us to teach, witness, welcome, comfort—and all the other things churches do. Yet he lets us work with him with the power of the Spirit to do these things. This is truly a privilege, an exciting adventure. In addition, it is a need all Christians have, even if they are unaware of it (Trumbauer 1995). When ministry is presented this way, even thankless jobs are done enthusiastically by joy-filled Christians aware of what the Lord has done for them.

It is important to remember the words of Scripture telling us that the Lord has provided all the gifts needed for his body, the church, to grow into the fullness of Christ (Eph. 4:11–13). This means that members of the church have already been given the very gifts needed to bring about growth. It's not a matter of begging people to give time, but of empowering people to use the gifts they have been given.

Unfortunately, many people do not think they have any

abilities to offer. Helping individuals discover the gifts they have, therefore, is one of the main challenges church leaders undertake in fulfilling their congregation's innate need for competence. In the long run, it is far more profitable for the church's leaders to spend time helping others discover their gifts than to spend time twisting the arms of those who are already overinvolved in ministry. An excellent resource in this regard is Sherry Weddell's audio course *The Called and Gifted Workshop* (Weddell and Sweeney 1998). Having gathered resources from Christian denominations throughout the country, she has developed an excellent tool to help people discern the gifts the Lord has given them. Once people begin to feel comfortable using these gifts for the building up of the body of Christ, they will also experience fulfillment in the need for competence, thus helping them grow spiritually while the church community profits from this newfound, enthusiastic sharing.

In this regard, church leaders are challenged to overcome what often appears to be an institutional hesitation to use the gifts and talents of its members, thus stifling the fulfillment of the people's need for competence. Perhaps it's a matter of control or power or insecurity. Maybe it's a fear that the person may not be able to perform the task. Regardless, if we fail to fulfill the need of our people to grow spiritually, we will limit the vitality of our churches.

6. Consider No Task for the Lord as Menial

Some individuals feel totally inadequate in terms of their ability to make a meaningful contribution to the church's life. Perhaps this is felt most when a significant portion of the congregation has limited education or works at jobs offering little satisfaction. A poor self-image fostered by a less than affirming cultural milieu can easily stymie an individual's growth. In striving to help people fulfill the need for competence, therefore, it is helpful for church leaders to recognize the hidden gifts that people bring to a situation—gifts that truly affect people's lives when they are offered. For example, one church began a "Martha and Mary" ministry, which provided hot meals several times a month to families experiencing unexpected illness that required hospital care. Hundreds of individuals who never saw their cooking ability as a Spirit-filled gift that could benefit others now found themselves serving in a significant and Gospel-centered way. Other congregations have "Handy Helpers" groups in which church members adept at fixing things are available to senior citizens with no family members present to take care of small problems like broken doors and leaky faucets. These men and women, many with little formal education, experience a genuine sense of accomplishment, realizing that their efforts make a difference.

To help incorporate more members into the work of feeding the poor, one congregation started a "Peanut Butter Ministry," making peanut butter and jelly sandwiches for a soup kitchen. Entire families—kids included—offer their services for several hours a month. The hope was to involve as many people as possible in feeding the poor rather than having the responsibility delegated to a paid social service director. The church reports that these simple endeavors have surpassed all expectations and, in the process, have helped individuals and entire families fulfill their need for competence. They were making a difference, and for them this made all the difference in the world.

7. Use Lay Witnesses during Sunday Services and Church Gatherings

Evangelization is the primary mission of any Christian church. Without a continuing proclamation of the Gospel and its accompanying invitation for others to "come and see," a church community easily withers and dies. In the Catholic tradition, a strong statement in this regard was made by Pope Paul VI in his Apostolic Exhortation *On Evangelization in the Modern World*, which stated that evangelization was the church's very identity (Paul VI 1975). Those who take the step of incorporating the Great Commission into their life find that it both energizes and renews them in their own faith. In short, it fulfills the need for competence.

Unfortunately, in our "politically correct" society, Christians today tend to shy away from sharing their faith publicly, much less inviting someone to come to a personal relationship with the Lord. There is a need (literally a survival need) for church leaders to show their members *how* to share the faith with others. This can be done by having individual church members give a brief, five-minute witness at a Sunday service. The fruit of this effort is manifold. It shows the congregation how to give a basic witness by highlighting within a brief period of time the core elements needed. The congregation itself is also edified as it hears one of its members share his or her story of faith. Finally, the person doing the sharing experiences great fulfillment in giving testimony to God's grace and in realizing some hearts may be touched. Churches that do this routinely, often at special services (for example, Ash Wednesday or adult baptisms) and informal gatherings (for example, men's and women's groups, teacher training sessions), report an increase in the number of people who now freely and willingly share their faith with non–church members, especially family members and co-workers.

8. Invite a Member to Participate in a Church Project by Writing a Personal "Letter of Call"

Receiving a personalized "letter of call" can help fulfill an individual's need for competence. In writing such an invitation, the church leader offers various reasons why a particular individual appears suited for a specific task. In addition, possible growth experiences associated with the task are also stated. The person who receives the letter has his or her gifts clearly affirmed and is reminded to pursue continual growth. Experience has shown that even if the individual decides not to accept the leader's request, the need for competence is satisfied, at least in part (see the sample "letter of call" in appendix 2, p. 125).

9. Incorporate a "Study Period" into Your Church's Staff Meeting

Too often church leaders fail to fulfill their own personal need for competence. With the demands of ministry, it becomes all too easy for leaders to ignore their own need for growth, forgetting that leaders also must ask the question, "Am I growing spiritually?" In order to meet this need, one pastor divided his staff's meeting time into three sections: prayer and faith-sharing, study, and business. The prayer and faith-sharing experience incorporated the suggestion noted in no. 2 on p. 43 above. During the study section the staff members discussed an article that had been assigned for reading. Staff members are responsible for arranging the prayer time and distributing an appropriate article several days before the scheduled meeting. In this way, members of the staff continued to grow as they shared input from areas of ministry which were not their main focus or expertise. Important exchanges of ideas led to sharing opportunities with members of the congregation, thus helping others fulfill their need for competence.

10. Recognize Unexpected Channels for Growth

Many church tasks offer additional growth benefits. Acquiring new skills in our ever-changing economy is essential for survival, and volunteering in an unfamiliar area is an opportunity to do so. A young teacher developed a talent for fund-raising by assisting a professional member who was conducting a building drive in her church. An older clerk learned computer software skills while assisting with the production of the weekly bulletin. Students satisfied community service assignments by helping run vacation Bible schools in Mexico. Even the networking that occurs naturally in church groups mixes people across occupations and industries, allowing for new employers and customers.

Reflection Questions

Use the following questions as a way to apply to your own church situation this theory of intrinsic motivation, particularly with regard to the need for competence. The purpose of the examples given above is not to have you duplicate what others have done. Rather, it's to help you see with a different set of eyes so you can identify ways that your church can fulfill the need for competence in its members.

- On the basis of your understanding of intrinsic motivation, identify three areas in your church where the need for competence is being fulfilled.
- On the basis of your understanding of intrinsic motivation, list three additional ways your church can fulfill its members' need for competence.
- Describe a recent personal experience that fulfilled your own need for competence.
- Identify a recent church project that probably frustrated a church member's need for competence. What was the cause of the frustration?
- Identify an upcoming church project for which you can use "letters of call" to invite individuals to participate.

Chapter Four

The Need for Relatedness

It is not good for the man to be alone.
— Genesis 2:18 NIV

"Sometimes we want to go where everybody knows your name" is the catchy line from the theme song of yesterday's hit TV situation comedy *Cheers*. It's frightening to think, however, that, for some, bars do a better job than churches of meeting the need to feel known and cared for.

To be in relationship with another is a profound human need. We want to care for others, and be cared for by them in return. It's why we give to charity and help a lost child. We were designed as social beings. Throughout his ministry, Jesus experienced this social dimension as he enjoyed the companionship of an inner group, confidants to whom he could turn in good times and bad. He performed his first public miracle at a major social occasion, the wedding feast at Cana. Later, he sent off his disciples "two by two" (Mark 6:7).

While families would seem to be the natural place to experience this closeness, the American penchant for geographic movement and the high rate of divorce have made physical proximity to family difficult, if not impossible for many. (Despite the ads, long-distance calls and e-mail do not approach "just like being there.") Yet even under ideal family circumstances, the church represents a great opportunity to meet this profound psychological need for connectedness. After all, believers have in common the most important person in life,

Jesus, and we all pray to the same heavenly Father guided by the same Holy Spirit.

Ideally, your church is one in which even the stranger who stops in experiences God's love among fellow worshipers. One woman put it this way: "I went to mass in Albuquerque, and when I slid into the pew, the woman next to me said: 'Hi, I don't believe I've seen you here before.' I felt so welcomed! When she and her husband learned I was from out of town, they said after mass they'd give me ideas on places to see. Later they introduced me to the priest. It made the worship experience so personal for me."

Feeling Connected

The second leg of Deci and Ryan's theory of intrinsic motivation is the need for relatedness: establishing a sense of mutual respect and reliance with others. This drive is seen in our joining groups or clubs, acting as good neighbors, and giving to charities. It explains why the acceptance and approval of others matter so much, and why nonreceptivity often hurts.

In today's society, the term "family" often carries a variety of meanings. For some, it refers to any configuration living in a household, regardless of natural or legal ties. Others use the term to describe the relationship existing within a close-knit group of friends. Many corporations often refer to employees as "family"—even as they implement downsizing to boost their market value. It is no stretch of the term, however, when it is applied to that body of believers called a congregation or church. Feeling connected—to God, his people, and his church—is a clear manifestation of the need for relatedness. Contrary to that need is feeling like an outsider when attending church. There are some houses of worship that mimic a pretentious country club where members come prepared to discuss their resumé in causal conversation at the coffee hour. What a sharp contrast to the model Jesus offered us: he dined with the "outest" of the outcasts, including a turncoat tax collector; he washed the feet of fishermen; he spoke with prostitutes, who could hear in his response a genuine sense of caring.

Because church communities offer an important way to meet the need for relatedness, church leaders are challenged to embrace an ongoing type of self-evaluation. Is this church "user friendly"? Is there a genuine welcome for all, no matter where they are on their spiritual journeys? Are their doubts as welcome as their beliefs? One church reported the tale of a mid-thirties fellow giving his personal testimony to the congregation before he was baptized. "You may recognize me as the guy who always sat back there—by the door. I did it for a reason. I didn't believe all this stuff about Christianity. But you always welcomed me here, and to your meetings and discussions. If one of you had 'come at me' to believe what you did, I would have been out that door like a bullet. But you accepted me where I was. Now I can honestly call you brothers and sisters, and sit up front." This church met the man's psychological need for relatedness and, in the process, his need for salvation.

Feeling isolated at church, being left out by "insiders" who regularly convene after the service, or experiencing only superficial greetings from fellow worshipers or the priest or minister all reveal an unmet need in this dimension of motivation.

Relatedness at Church: Supports and Frustrations

We present a list of experiences that have been helpful in meeting the need for relatedness in a church community. You'll note that there is nothing extraordinary here. In a certain sense, it's all very obvious. The fact is, however, that church leaders sometimes let the obvious slip by as they engage in the many details of ministerial service.

In reviewing these examples and reflecting on your own church situation in terms of meeting the need for relatedness, you probably will become more aware of how often we as church leaders unwittingly disappoint, exclude, reject, or fail in our attempts to fulfill a person's need for relatedness. Sometimes being more aware of personal relationships can rectify the situation. Apologies, of course, always help. At other times, however, church leaders may have to correct an employee or church volunteer who repeatedly "drops the ball" in this area. To help in such situations, chapters 6 and 7 on employees' motivation and psychological fusion may prove useful.

Finally, remember to think "long term." It can take some time before you begin to see a significant difference. One pastor noted that as his co-workers began to embrace this approach (consciously or unconsciously following his example), the power of intrinsic motivation was released within more and more members. In turn, this experience filtered throughout the congregation.

But regardless of top leadership's acceptance, *you* can make a difference in your ministry—starting today.

1. Promote Connection at Your Worship Service

Large gatherings typically foster a subconscious distancing from one another to create "personal space." Yet the worship experience offers a ready means to begin breaking down this barrier. As the service begins, the minister, priest, or music director can extend a warm welcome and suggest taking a minute for everyone to introduce themselves to those nearby. If there is a point in your worship tradition when children go to their own service in another part of the church, use a caring tone with them. "At this time the children are invited to their own worship service downstairs" is a lot more welcoming than "The children are now dismissed."

If there appear to be visitors in church, greet them from the pulpit, expressing gratitude that they are worshiping with this church family today and the hope that they sense God's presence. "If you are visiting today, please know you are most welcome here." Expressed enthusiastically, this type of invitation puts people at ease and connects them with the community's experience of worship.

At one church the music director has become an important part of this process. Before announcing the gathering song, he welcomes visitors as well as the congregation, expressing gratitude that they are worshiping with the church family. The invitation is very simple: "If you're visiting our church today, welcome; if you are looking for a church family, please introduce yourself to one of our ushers."

Since one of the biggest concerns of the unchurched is that "all churches care about is money," some churches choose to announce to visitors: "The collection we will take later is the concern of our church membership, so feel free to pass the basket along. We would invite you, however, to fill out the visitors card found in your pew and deposit it in the basket at that time."

2. Engage the Heart with Music

Advertisers have long known the emotional impact the right music can have on listeners. Evangelical congregations are particularly good at getting everyone to sing songs and hymns that prepare the heart for the sermon. Such songs might be termed "affective," in the sense that Jonathan Edwards speaks of religious experience. Besides providing an opportunity to prepare hearts for the message to be preached that day, there is something intimate about singing with others. Unfortunately, many Roman Catholic and mainline Protestant congregations still struggle in this regard, possibly because of the type of music chosen.

On a practical level, take care that an amplified cantor's voice or musical instrument does not dominate the sound in the building. If people cannot hear themselves sing, they won't. Most important of all, don't skimp on a sound system. You'd be amazed what a difference a good musical environment makes.

The goal, of course, is to have everyone feel they belong and are able to participate. Choosing songs and hymns that are singable, having a copy of the words and music (legally reproduced), directing everyone to the right page in the hymnal are details that add up to a big welcome. Granted, striking the balance between familiar favorites and interesting new pieces is often difficult. Nevertheless, the music should engage the participants, keep up interest (see the need for competence), and diminish boredom.

3. Greet Each Individual Personally on Arrival and Departure

Select and train ushers to welcome and assist those arriving, person by person. Eye contact, a handshake, and a personal greeting go a long way in developing relatedness within a congregation. "Hope it's a great service for you this morning," "Good to see you," "Happy Lord's Day," "Hi, I'm Paul" are simple examples of *personal* greetings that could be extended. If the greeter knows the individual, an expression of care about some known concern—"I've been praying for you"—is the stuff of agape love. If you have complex parking problems, put a greeter out in the lot and, on rainy Sundays, another at the curb with a big umbrella.

Ministers and priests who greet attendees after each service help set an atmosphere that enables members to feel connected. To maximize contact, be firm but gentle in helping overly talkative members conclude their conversation or else the marginal member or a visitor will slip by silently. As for the enthusiastic if somewhat dominant speakers, tactfully interrupt them and offer a phone call during the week to hear more about what they wish to say. Better to risk a slight offense to the regular attendee than fail to greet the visitor or less familiar member.

Another opportunity for priests and ministers to support the need for relatedness is at the close of the service: "If you have any questions or thoughts about today's sermon, or if you want to discuss your relationship with God, there is nothing more important you or I have to do. Please feel free to call me during the week and we'll talk." If something preached or taught has sparked a response, make it easy for the hearer to act on that stirring rather than dismiss it as a momentary emotional experience. In doing this you reinforce the fact that religion involves a relationship with God and God's people, and we don't have to go it alone. In a similar vein, a deacon at one church invites anyone who needs special prayer to meet him immediately after the service so they can pray together. Being available in this way helps people connect, reminds them that their relationship with God involves others, and fulfills in a tangible manner people's need to relate, to be touched, and to be cared for.

4. Build a Genuine Sense of Family

Offering opportunities to care for each other's needs, particularly at critical times in members' lives, fosters a familial experience of intimacy. For example, some churches have volunteers who deliver complete family dinners for the weeks following a mother's giving birth or a member's return from a hospital stay for any reason. Other congregations establish special funds for meeting emergency financial needs of members. One church we know has had a great deal of success with its Ministry of Hope, helping the bereaved know they are part of an extended church family (Aridas 1998).

Sunday bulletins are simple communication devices for sharing the highlights and needs of church families, including sections for "Celebrating God's blessings" (births, marriages, etc.) and "We are praying for...." (illnesses). Similarly, annual Ministry Fairs permit the identification of ways people in the church already are reaching out to meet the needs of the community. Church directories are another important means for getting to know each other better, particularly if photos are included, an inexpensive proposition with today's technology. If yours is a large congregation, updates can be issued as supplements ("We welcome...") each half year or so.

5. Encourage Formal and Informal Groups

There's nothing new about church picnics, potluck dinners, or fund-raising bake sales. But do not discount other, more intimate initiatives.

One church established an Ironman series for men, borrowing from Proverbs 27:17 NIV: "As iron sharpens iron, so one man sharpens another." This small church grew in numbers as its winter Saturday morning series grew in reputation. (Saturday mornings in winter were chosen specifically since the time was free of the team sports that compete for a father's attention in other seasons of the year.) Its format was simple: speak to the concerns of men wishing to live a Christian life. Intended as a service to all men in the community, this band of ten grew over the years to over a hundred men, the majority of whom came from other churches or had no church affiliation. Its advertising secret? Simple invitations, one friend to another, augmented by a yearly press release and ad. Many of these individuals went back to their own churches with their faith strengthened, some even starting Bible studies in their own congregations. This ministry proved so successful that the women of the church followed suit with a series of Bible studies geared to the concerns of wives, mothers, and single women.

Church researchers repeatedly affirm this type of strategy: small groups, for discussions as well as Bible study, prove essential in promoting a sense of connectedness with a church.

6. Deal Everyone In on What's Going On

It is true of nearly every institution, including churches: there are those who feel only marginally involved. It's an organizational fact of life. Before getting comfortable with the "It's their own fault!" retort, however, we can respond to these feelings from the vantage point of intrinsic motivation. What can we do to present an inviting, engaging environment that counteracts this organizational inclination?

"Keep all things in the light" captures the notion that leaders should share their special knowledge whenever feasible. That goes from providing information about the budgeting process to plans for new ministries. One pastor writes a monthly letter to the members of his congregation, explaining what has happened over the previous month and what concerns face the parish in the coming month. He gives figures, dollar amounts, projections, and statistics whenever possible. Does everyone read these letters? Probably not, but those who do feel connected, their need for relatedness fulfilled. Such endeavors may make life more complicated as members of the community raise unexpected questions, but the alternative is to remain satisfied with the feeling of "us and them."

Every church has special events that draw a lot of "outsiders"—people from other religious traditions as well as many unchurched persons. Weddings, funerals, and baptisms are a few prominent examples. How inviting is that experience? Do these visitors know what is going on, and why? We take for granted they know how to locate the hymns or Scripture text, when to sit or stand, what prayers are said. Simple directions go a long way in fulfilling a visitor's need to connect. "Please turn to page 52 as we sing together our response to God's Word." "Please stand as we read...." These directions seem obvious to the initiated, but without them visitors easily can think they are lost in a foreign land.

7. Become Seeker-Friendly

Best-selling author and pastor Rick Warren, of Saddleback Church in California, states with humor that we Christians invite the unchurched to come and sit on seventeenth-century chairs (pews), sing eighteenth-century songs (hymns), and listen to a nineteenth-century instrument (organ) (Warren 1995). And these visitors (for some reason) think we are not relevant to their contemporary concerns! "No, duh," our youth might well respond.

While over 80 percent of Americans profess to believe in the God of the Bible, fewer than 25 percent will be found in church on any given Sunday (Hadaway 1993). (Don't be misled by popular polls suggesting a much higher percentage: such statistics can be attributed to what researchers call "socially desirable" responses in surveys). Regardless of your denomination's theological position on this, that is, whether attendance is mandatory, all certainly can agree that non-attendance diminishes people's opportunity for growth in their relationship with God.

In many denominations, therefore, a majority of adults are disconnected from the body of Christ. (Happily there are dramatic exceptions: churches that tap into intrinsic motivation.) When they show up at a service, such as Christmas or Easter, they rightly can be called "seekers." They may not know what it is they are looking for, but they've come to the right place. They have a chance to connect with God and his people.

One thing we can do is to take some of the unnecessary mystique out of our service. This does not mean "dumbing down" or making things less reverential, but merely explaining what's going on to those less familiar. One author observed a painfully missed opportunity. At a funeral service for a prominent local educator, about a third of the packed assembly were Jewish colleagues and friends. The pastor leading the service, however, continually used denominational jargon without any explanation. Undoubtedly, the preacher felt he was being faithful to the Gospel, using the phrases that made sense to his usual constituency. Unfortunately, he wasn't speaking to the group sitting in front of him. Although Christians believe the New Testament is the Old Testament fulfilled, this pastor seemed to have had no intention of helping his Jewish audience consider that possibility for their own lives.

A study by the Barna Research Group suggests that churches may be missing the mark on friendliness (Barna 2000b). In a study of four thousand churches called during business hours, only one-third of those called responded with a human being available on the first call. Despite as many as twelve call attempts, Barna reports that 40 percent of the churches never provided contact with a live person. This highlights the importance of the receptionist in a church. To become seeker-friendly, therefore, it remains important to handle every call as the call of a seeker. Whether the caller is a member simply asking for the time of a meeting, a stranger newly moved into the area, a person in distress needing housing or food, or a person in crisis requiring special ministry, the receptionist is the first line of contact. The receptionist's helpful response makes all the difference in the world. To "smile over the phone lines" is the goal for a seeker-friendly church intent on meeting the needs of relatedness that come its way.

8. Purpose after the Less Familiar

All too often, we handle problems with familiar or comfortable solutions. In doing so, however, we can ignore the creative power of the Spirit whose solution to many problems is not the one we would prefer or even imagine. "Purpose after the Less Familiar," therefore, encourages church leaders to "blue sky" for solutions with intrinsic motivation in mind, even though your initial thoughts might appear odd, strange, or even unworkable. For example, cliques may seem inevitable as people reach for easy conversation with familiar people after a service. As Christians, however, we are after more: "They will know that we are Christians by our love," we sing. One church creatively used its resources to address the problem of somewhat exclusive gatherings in the aisles after the service. The youth director encouraged his teenagers, who were all too familiar with the destructiveness of cliques, to go into the aisles after the service and speak with those who appeared to be alone. What a sight: kids with buzz-cuts and in jeans sharing their "like"-filled speech with elderly worshipers in their Sunday-best attire. Some meaningful relationships were established, and the students reported how they genuinely felt welcomed by these mature members of the congregation.

At another congregation, attempts to maintain a website continually fell apart. At the suggestion of a church member, however, the pastor contacted a shut-in paraplegic young adult and asked him to develop and maintain the site. In doing so, the young man's need for relatedness and competence was met, and the church members gained another avenue to build relatedness through an Internet presence. Interestingly enough, a Bible study group also developed at the young man's house, thereby increasing his connection to the community and allowing others to profit from their relationship with an extraordinary young Christian.

9. Build on Natural Moments of Encounter

In an ideal world, people would seek to celebrate baptisms or weddings at a church because they were believers and participants in the church community. In many Christian churches, however, that is not the case, as more and more "cultural Christians" present their children for baptism even though the parents themselves have little or no contact with the church. The same is true of marriage. In some denominations the case is very simple: the celebration is not permitted. Other Christian churches, however, view the situation differently. Since the scope of this book does not permit a discussion on this topic, we wish to address those church communities that do encounter this situation, suggesting how they might use it to fulfill a need for relatedness.

At one parish, more than two hundred infant baptisms took place in a year. Conservatively speaking, more than half of the families who presented their child for baptism had little or no contact with the parish community. A large percentage of the parents were unmarried or involved in a second or third marriage. For many years, the parish based its baptism instruction on a classroom model, that is, someone spoke at the parent or parents for about an hour, giving them a theological explanation of baptism while reminding them of their responsibility to bring the child up according to the Gospel. The instruction sometimes included a filmstrip or video presentation. Beginning several years ago, however, another approach has been taken—one that has already begun to bear fruit. Rather than a lengthy theological presentation, three brief presentations are given: a welcome and an overview of the sacrament, a personal witness story of how faith has developed in a person's life, and a guided meditation that focuses on healing and reconciliation with the community. This model uses a small-group format, which encourages reflection and sharing among the couples themselves, guided by a parish-trained facilitator. Most important, however, is the assigning of mentors to each of the families. These are dedicated church members who promise to pray for the couples and remain in contact with them via notes and phone calls throughout the year. With the provision of mentors, the possibility for families not connected to the community to establish a church contact rose significantly.

Most important, this model highlights the efficacy of carrying out instruction in the context of a group rather than one-on-one. It is the rare church leader who can provide such instruction without communicating an "I-have-the-information-you-need" mentality, which impairs a sense of relatedness.

10. Be Ready to Give an Accounting of Your Hope (see 1 Peter 3:15)

The foundation for all of the above experiences rests in bringing the individual to a personal relationship with the Lord. This is not effectively done in any sort of rote fashion, for example, saying a particular prayer, but through relational ministry. Relational ministry necessarily includes helping people come to a conscious awareness of Jesus in their lives in order to fulfill completely their need for relatedness. Leaving the fulfillment of this need to a church community alone is simply not enough. In the end, that will disappoint. Likewise, it is inappropriate to assume that a personal relationship with Jesus apart from the community is consistent with the Lord's teaching. To satisfy the need for relatedness, people need a relationship with the Lord, nurtured and "fleshed out" by their relationships within the body of Christ. This is basic to church ministry and growth.

The apostle Peter reminds us to be prepared to share our reason for hope, that is, our experience of the Lord. Church leaders often shy away from this kind of witness, fearing that they will turn people away. When done properly, however, our personal sharing really invites others to turn toward the One who ultimately fulfills our need for relatedness. This does not mean that we preach at others. Quite the contrary. A simple, personal sharing of faith helps people realize that a relationship with the God who is revealed in Christ is truly possible, and that Jesus' death and resurrection have reconciled us sinners to our Father. In that sharing we also express the truth that this restored relationship develops fully in the community of believers called church.

Reflection Questions

Use the following questions as a way of making practical in your own church situation the theory of intrinsic motivation with regard to fulfilling the need for relatedness.

- On the basis of your understanding of intrinsic motivation, identify three areas in your church where the need for relatedness is being fulfilled.

- On the basis of your understanding of intrinsic motivation, list three additional ways your church can fulfill its members' need for relatedness.

- Describe a recent personal experience that fulfilled *your* need for relatedness.

- Identify a church ministry that recently fulfilled a church member's need for relatedness. What elements in that program facilitated this success?

- Identify a current church ministry that does not fulfill a person's need for relatedness. List three possible ways you can rectify the situation.

- Identify a recent encounter where you had the opportunity to share a personal experience of faith with a person with whom you came in contact. What was the result of that sharing for you and for the other person?

Chapter Five

The Need for Autonomy

You are free to eat from any tree in the garden.
— Genesis 2:16 NIV

It's funny how we like to buy things, yet hate to be *sold* them. The dynamic is not unlike the corporate truism: "A plan imposed is a plan opposed."

To be free is a conspicuous human need. Sometimes this need is evinced quite dramatically: a family sets out in the dead of night from Cuba and heads on a skimpy boat to the U.S. coastline—just to be free. Other times the quest is more subtle: an employee leaves for another firm because he can no longer stand being "micromanaged" by his supervisor.

But are people in a church concerned with freedom? You bet. The coercion of the harried pastor asking a member, yet again, "Please head up the annual drive again, as a special favor to me...Okay?" Or the appeal letter offering an enticement for giving: "A $1,000 gift ranks you a Gold-level Donor on the Bishop's Council list!" Such appeals are extrinsic in nature: the *focus* is on something apart from the purpose behind the request or event. To give because one truly believes in the mission or the need is to act, with personal conviction, on the basis of an intrinsic motivation. Giving in that mode is not only nonpressured; it is usually more generous.

Over a ten-year period, one church enjoyed such remarkable growth that it needed three times its current space for Sunday morning worship services. Its fund-raising campaign consisted of several Sunday morning messages on biblical stewardship and a brochure bearing the motto: "Providing a seat in which someone might come to know the love of God." All pledges were confidential, known only to the church's treasurer. Not even the pastor knew of individuals' contributions. The total amount pledged far exceeded the desired down payment for the expansion. And the amount finally collected surpassed the amount initially pledged.

Although contributions differed, people appeared to be giving with equal sacrifice. Some gave of their relatively humble savings; families deferred vacations and home expansions. All who gave truly believed that the building expansion was the opportunity to help others discover God's love for them. This belief motivated members to support the cause since they were convinced that nothing was more important than providing a place where a person could experience God's love. The pastor's role was simple: present the need, articulate God's teaching with regard to stewardship, and minister to all who came. He did not have to urge, cajole, or shame members into giving.

The Need for Autonomy

The third leg of Deci and Ryan's theory of intrinsic motivation is the need for autonomy, the need to experience some level of control or self-determination in our endeavors. Autonomy is about having a sense of choice, feeling like the initiator of our own actions or involvement. It necessarily excludes being coerced, seduced, or cajoled into doing something. "Empowerment" is the relevant cliché in the workforce; the same concept appears as "ownership" in our school systems. We find biblical support for this need for autonomy in Genesis when God endows humanity with choice, even to go our own sinful way.

Some churches "max out" on giving people autonomy: "Write your own creed here!" They miss the point. Meeting a person's need for autonomy does not mean we do not talk about sin, or challenge immoral behavior, or correct wrongdoing, or state clearly the church's creed. Nor does it require a liberalization of church beliefs, rules, or values. For example, one research study (Baard 1994a) on evangelical Protestants reported very high levels of the experience of autonomy at church even while the church maintained its traditional teaching of strict obedience to the dictates of Scripture.

One elder in a mainline Protestant church decided to "work with the system" when he encountered an institutional problem. Participating with the other elders in an examination of candidates for confirmation, he sensed that it was pretty much a ceremonial ritual for the half-dozen teenagers present. The leader declared to the candidates, "This ceremony is intended to affirm the fact that this religion, Christianity, is now formally *your* religion, not just one handed to you by your parents. It means that you truly believe Christ died for *your* sins, not just for those of the world." The elder further explained that a personal relationship with Jesus involves far more than a religious ceremony and concluded by encouraging the young people to look forward to such an experience one day. For some in the group of candidates, hopefully, it was an affirmation that things were now different: they would take their rightful, responsible place in the congregation and look forward to maturing in their walk with Christ. For the rest, at least they now knew that the matter meant more than simply a ceremony. We submit that one reason so many post-confirmation and post–bar mitzvah and post–bas mitzvah teens drop out of church or synagogue soon after these public ceremonies is a sense of being coerced into the ritual.

Meeting the need for autonomy can be as simple as acknowledging that whether to do or not to do something is our decision to make. Even volunteer soldiers in the military report high levels of autonomy: they chose to be there, and when the chips are down—in a fighting situation—they know they will have considerable authority to make decisions.

Some may mistake this as a call for permissiveness. The choice to obey or not, however, is one Jesus often extended. In Mark 10:17 a rich young man asked, "What must I do to inherit eternal life?" Knowing this young man's love of his possessions was getting in the way of his relationship with God, Jesus instructed him to "sell what you have and give to the poor." But the man became very sad and walked away.

Jesus didn't try to convince the young man to change his decision. He respected the young man's freedom to choose, even though he chose the wrong path. The idea of autonomy is behind the expression: God has no grandchildren. Each of us must decide personally to turn to the Lord, or not to. Those who do become "children of God" (John 1:12).

Autonomy at Church: Supports and Frustrations

We now will look at selected opportunities to address this need for autonomy, or self-determination, in local churches. We offer these examples to encourage your own pastoral creativity in satisfying this need and avoiding its frustration in your church.

1. Nurture Active Collaboration in Church Activities

Respondents to surveys on church motivation report great satisfaction when they feel they have a chance to influence how things are done. Some churches use an occasional questionnaire to solicit input and feedback from members, for example, on the times of services or the possibility of expanding ministries. Such a survey could be inserted in the weekly bulletin or included with a general mailing to update members on church affairs (which supports members' need for relatedness as well). The increasing popularity of church websites provides an additional venue for gathering this type of information. Any attempt, no matter how small, helps satisfy this need for autonomy. Full validation of the process, however, requires church leaders to convey to the congregation the survey's result, and any decisions based on the input submitted.

Unfortunately, a fear of surrendering control often inhibits church leaders from cultivating what industry and education have discovered will help them achieve their goal—motivated participants. At other times, leaders do not seek input because they fear offending *some* people if they are unable to accommodate every request. In the end, of course, the leaders offend *all* the people by not including them. Unquestionably, empowerment of the members is a major challenge facing church leaders, especially since the days of autocratic management are diminishing quickly in every institution.

One author had this technique of collaborative decision-making work quite well in a difficult situation. His parish was preparing for the possible loss of service of a retired priest. This would require a reduction in the daily mass schedule, a very sensitive matter to those whose lifelong Catholic experience always included several options for attending daily mass. Rather than deciding unilaterally whether the 8:00 A.M. or the 9:00 A.M. daily mass would be discontinued, the pastor held several meetings with those who attended those services. Through collaborative problem-solving, a consensus was reached: a Solomon-like decision to keep the 8:00 A.M. mass on three days and the 9:00 A.M. mass on three others. All were satisfied that their voices were heard and their needs considered in making the decision.

What occurs when "no" must be the answer, despite an inclusive effort? In terms of preserving the need for autonomy, a sensitive response goes a long way. "Regrettably, we are unable to..." is a legitimate outcome when all are faithful to the process. It behooves pastoral leaders to invite input only when the participants' opinions can truly influence the decision-making process. For example, to initiate discussion of a topic with a church council when an autonomous decision is not possible is self-defeating.

2. Invite Rather Than Pressure

Our choice of words subtly communicates our desire either to control or to respect a listener's autonomy. "I believe the best thing for you to do..." is an example of an assertive communication. "You should..." is experienced as aggressive and controlling and almost automatically resisted. Presenting a need in a noncontrolling manner appeals to the listeners' desire for autonomy; they are making their decisions volitionally. Similarly, offering admonishment in a "shoulding" manner may evoke compliance, but not acceptance. There is a fine line between urging fellow Christians to conform to a Scripture-based pattern of behavior, and emotionally manipulating people with guilt to shape their compliance.

As for the matter of recruiting volunteers, the arm-twisting techniques of years ago are giving way to an approach that supports autonomy: "John, our newcomers group needs a leader for the fall. I have watched you keep an eye out for visitors each week. Would you consider whether this is a gift you'd like to share in the growth of our church?" And then the invitor *must genuinely let go,* thus respecting John, who must come to his own decision.

In the area of finances, when there are urgent needs, bringing them candidly to the congregation is far more effective than beating around the bush. Even better, however, is to do so in terms of a biblical mandate, leading individuals to listen prayerfully to God about financial stewardship (Champlin 1997). Introducing the biblical understanding of tithing has brought great success in the churches we've researched. A mandate from God appears to conflict less with a person's autonomy than an urging by church authorities. The result of this self-determining approach can be the elimination of additional fees, second collections, Las Vegas Nights, bingo, etc.

3. Acknowledge Rather Than Manipulate

We all like to feel our contributions are appreciated. An occasional note from a church leader does wonders. Making a conscious effort to say "Thank you" to all who offered themselves in service to others also goes a long way toward affirming a person's impact. Another way to acknowledge service by a person or a committee is to include a notice in the weekly bulletin, perhaps under a "Time and Talent" column, in which you acknowledge God's grace working through individuals who are serving in various ways. For example, one church uses this basic formula: "With thanks to God for the time and talents shared by our members, we acknowledge the work done by _____ in providing last Sunday's Creative Praise Night, which highlighted our kids' choir and dance ministries. Our children were taught an important stewardship lesson, namely, how to use their gifts to serve God and bring enjoyment to others in the process." In taking this approach, the generous offer of service is the focus rather than personal promotion. We do, however, offer a caution: if acknowledgments of individuals who made an event possible are overdone, such as in a press release, you risk shifting the focus of contribution from an intrinsic to an extrinsic one.

A line is crossed when a leader uses arm-twisting to get more out of volunteers or contributors. We can subtly shame people into bringing an offering up to a higher level or volunteering for a task, but that will very likely undermine their long-term, intrinsic "I believe in this" motivation. In addition, the research also suggests that an extrinsically motivated individual will not display nearly as much persistence and creativity in the task as will an intrinsically motivated person. In the same vein, enticing volunteers or contributors with extrinsic rewards—plaques, gifts, names on pews—can undermine what may have been intrinsic motivation toward the activity to start with (Kohn 1993). In such cases the church leader needs to distinguish between a gesture of thanks and a reward.

4. Permit Freedom of Expression

Although many denominations have limited latitude in applying church rules, there is no need to eliminate people's right to express their opinion about a policy. Beginning a response with "I can understand your concerns about this teaching; however, as we seek to understand..." is easier to hear than "You shouldn't feel that way." The former preserves a person's autonomy (the freedom to believe); the latter just asserts the speaker's (or institution's) authority over the listener. This is not mere semantics, nor does it call into question a church's authority over matters affecting its members. It is to encourage communicating in a manner that brings about motivated understanding rather than manipulated compliance. In taking this approach, church leaders are able to make the most of their unique opportunity to help members reconcile their natural desire to do their own thing with their spiritual need to conform to God's will for their lives.

It is not unusual for church leaders to get letters complaining about a particular situation. Responding to all signed letters in some fashion is important, always thanking the writers for their thoughts even if the leaders do not intend to follow their suggestions. This is critical in areas of church policy when an individual does not agree with the pastoral approach embraced by a church leader.

5. Encourage a Sense of Volition Regarding Church Rituals

Support for autonomy is sometimes an institutional matter. When church, social, or parental pressures force people to take a particular step of faith, the experience effectively frustrates their need to choose freely what they do. Several typical situations come to mind: a parent presenting a child for baptism because the grandparents expect the youngster to be christened; an unbelieving couple seeking a church wedding because "that's what my parents want." In these cases, people approach the church for the celebration of a ritual when they have not freely chosen to make the implicit statement of faith behind it.

This process is painfully evident in many adolescents' experiences in Christian churches (see the Church Engagement Model chart, figure 1, p. 27 above). In some Christian denominations, the celebration of confirmation supposedly affirms a young person's "adult" acceptance of the Christian faith. More often than not, however, the confirmation candidates' pledge that "this is now my religion," becomes their personal exodus from church practice for the years ahead. (The same is true, we are told, in Judaism, where there is a great drop-off in attendance following the bar and bas mitzvah.) In effect, by exerting social pressure to conform, churches and parents sometimes serve to negate the very thing they were after: acceptance of the faith. When truly free to decide after the obligatory ritual, these young men and women walk away from their churches. These observations are certainly not meant to criticize denominations that find themselves in this situation. The fact is, most Christian churches confront these situations on an almost daily basis. We are simply stating the consequences that such practices engender. According to the research of motivational theorists, the result of such practices probably will be amotivation, or extrinsic motivation at best. If we stay this course, the long-term projection is frightening: churches with amotivated members with little desire to support the church's life and mission.

Although the situation is daunting in that we are dealing with an age group that is often rebellious against any type of authority, there are steps we can take. We can help young people make an age-appropriate response to the ritual they are celebrating. For example, strive to respond to the faith questions that the students have at this time in their lives. Remember, however, that they will not be the same faith questions that adult leaders have. Make every effort to preserve the sense that taking a step in faith by celebrating the ritual is a decision that only they can make. Helping adolescents respond in faith takes a great deal of time and effort on the part of the church community. We maintain, however, that this expenditure is one of the best investments a church can make, even if the results may not seem apparent at first.

6. Include Staff Members in Running Staff Meetings

Not all people enjoy meetings, and this seems especially true of a church's staff. Meetings are often boring, repetitive, controlling, and not very productive. A primary reason is that most pastors or priests have never been trained to run staff meetings. Lacking such preparation, they default to the idea that a staff meeting is meant to cover things that are on their mind or handle situations that they can no longer ignore. Run poorly, a meeting can often last over two hours, not the optimal attention span for today's citizens. How, then, might a staff meeting help fulfill a person's need for autonomy?

Keep the staff meeting within certain time limits. For most churches, it's doubtful that the business part of a staff meeting needs to go beyond sixty minutes. (If prayer and study are part of the meeting, additional time will be needed; see chapter 3, p. 43, for a description of such a meeting.) This assumes, of course, that the staff is meeting at least twice a month. However, if a situation arises when additional time is needed, the person leading the meeting can ask the staff's permission for a time extension, specifying the amount of time the meeting will continue. This small gesture gives members a choice to say yes or no. If they decide no, then it probably is best to end the meeting since the leader has lost them anyway.

Having staff members contribute or suggest modifications to the agenda for each meeting also supports the need for autonomy. This can be accomplished by distributing a planned agenda to staff members several days before the meeting and inviting comments. The person outlining the meeting (who need not be the pastor) places on the agenda only those items submitted beforehand. Thus the staff takes responsibility for its own meeting.

7. Foster Holiness

The paradox of dying to self in order to conform fully to the Spirit's life is the foundation of Christian freedom. It is our ultimate fulfillment, the complete satisfaction of our need for autonomy.

Church leaders have the responsibility and privilege of helping church members move beyond an initial spiritual awakening to maturity in Christ. Retreat days, spiritual direction, mentoring, discipleship programs, accountability groups, and other suggestions offered in chapter 3 all help foster the maturity to be truly free in Christ.

8. Incorporate Church Members into Task Forces

In today's face-paced society, many find themselves committed to a variety of activities that effectively eliminate their ability to offer much time for church matters. It's unfortunate because many of these busy members are the church's most valuable resource in terms of talent, education, and insight.

To minimize the time crunch, church leaders can utilize short-term committees, often called task forces. Members offer their gifts for a particular project with a clear time limit. For example, if you are seeking a new youth minister for the congregation, invite your resident human resources "expert" to join a small group of youth workers in devising a job description and recruitment plan. The youth workers acquire knowledge (satisfying their competence need), and the church member with the needed expertise influences the church's selection process (addressing the autonomy need).

At one Roman Catholic parish, the celebration of First Communion traditionally had been on Saturday morning, with friends and relatives being the primary participants. Having decided to move these celebrations to the parish's Sunday masses so the entire community could participate, the pastor organized a task force that incorporated a wide spectrum of church members. Ushers, parents, artists, musicians, and catechists devised the best possible celebration for the community, visiting other parishes in the area to gather ideas. Intrinsic motivation thrived as all three psychological needs were clearly met with this single effort.

9. Work with Volunteers to Develop a Specific Budget to Accomplish a Task

Once volunteers have accepted the invitation to participate on a church project, the leader's task in supporting their need for autonomy does not end. Sometimes the lack of direction or what seems to be a "free hand" can raise the volunteers' level of anxiety because they are not sure how far to proceed. An *optimal* level of autonomy is ideal: enough structure, enough freedom to move. This can be especially true in the area of finances. For example, Tom, having been asked by the youth minister to work with a teenage RAP ("Religion and People") group, gladly accepted. The youth minister met with Tom several times to trade ideas about a curriculum and calendar of youth activities; he also asked Tom to consider what expenses he might incur by running the meeting at his home. At first Tom didn't realize there would be any expenses, until the youth minister reminded him that teenagers can consume considerable quantities of snacks at their gatherings. There would be times when Tom might need to meet separately with one or two of the teens to discuss their concerns at a diner, which meant, of course, more food. Over the course of a year, the amount of money Tom spent ministering to the youth could be substantial. By helping Tom plan a budget, the youth minister helped fulfill Tom's need for autonomy (he gave him control of this part of the ministry), while preserving his need for competence (Tom wouldn't go broke before the end of the year). The same idea applies to many kinds of volunteer service: teachers need supplies for class, musicians need legal copies of music to distribute when they visit a nursing home, volunteer drivers who shuttle people to doctor visits need travel expenses. More often than not, people choose not to request payment for supplies, gas, and other expenses incurred when providing a volunteer service. Church leaders, however, meet the need for autonomy by acknowledging that money is spent in these areas, and the church, seeing the volunteers' service as a formal ministry, willingly accepts the attendant financial responsibility.

10. Organize "Town Hall" Meetings

Elected officials have had great success, at least from the standpoint of relating to their constituencies, in conducting some version of town hall meetings. The purpose is to provide a convenient, informal venue that allows people the opportunity to express themselves. Since some individuals, perhaps out of shyness or insecurity, hesitate to voice their concerns to church leaders, a town hall meeting affords them a secure environment in which their experience is heard and valued. Surrounded by their peers and stimulated by the discussion, these "silent members" now have a chance to express themselves—perhaps for the first time. To insure their participation and prevent them from getting lost in the crowd, strive to organize the meeting around small group participation, with each group reporting back to the main body after a specific time period of discussion has passed. Doing so prevents the more vocal from dominating the proceedings while allowing the less vocal an opportunity to share their thoughts without having to defend them before a large group.

As with all genuine attempts to empower the congregation, a town hall meeting implicitly commits the leadership to hear and respond to suggestions and concerns. This can be done through a written report published for the congregation. The meeting itself is not the place or the time for leaders to respond. The meeting is an opportunity for sharing ideas and concerns, not responding to or defending them.

A Final Observation

Of the three needs discussed—competence, relatedness, and autonomy—meeting people's need for autonomy is, by far, the most challenging. In terms of a church's well-being, however, it is vitally important. Take particular care, therefore, to remain sensitive to an individual's choice, just as Jesus always did. If anyone were capable of persuading another, it was Jesus, yet we read of no incident in the Gospels in which he pressured someone to believe a certain way. Avoid the temptation, so often facing church leadership, to be satisfied with extrinsic motivation that seems to offer an immediate

Figure 3. The Relationship between Types of Motivation

Observable behavior	IM....EM................	AM
Psychological proximity	IM................EM....	AM

IM = Intrinsic Motivation
EM = Extrinsic Motivation
AM = Amotivation

---

fix to a problem, for example, a budget needs to be covered, a class needs to be taught. Intrinsic or extrinsic—at least the matter gets addressed (observable behavior), we might easily say. Figure 3 above reminds us why this approach is counterproductive in the long run. For example, though the class might be taught, the lack of genuine volition places the volunteer closer to the amotivational state of mind (psychological proximity).

Even though behavior coming out of both intrinsic and extrinsic orientations may look the same, the psychological processes behind the two are very far apart. And the worst of all is that extrinsic motivation—because of the absence of autonomy support—easily slides over into amotivation. And that is where a church's death by suffocation begins. Many flee to "breathe freely."

Reflection Questions

These questions are offered to help you develop ways to meet your congregation's need for autonomy.

- On the basis of your understanding of intrinsic motivation, identify three situations where you helped to fulfill a member's need for autonomy.

- On the basis of your understanding of intrinsic motivation, list three additional ways you can help members fulfill their need for autonomy.
- Describe a recent personal experience that fulfilled *your* need for autonomy.
- Identify a church project that recently failed to fulfill a church volunteer's need for autonomy. What prevented its fulfillment?
- Identify a recent church program that fulfilled a church member's need for autonomy. What steps did you take to bring this about?

Chapter Six

Developing Motivated Employees

> *To ... be happy in [one's] work—*
> *this is a gift of God.*
> —Ecclesiastes 5:19 NIV

Keeping church employees content is always a challenge. And when an economy is robust with high-paying jobs, that challenge increases dramatically. A recent study of the corporate workplace (Baard, Deci, and Ryan 1999), however, pointed out the superiority of an intrinsic motivation approach to managing employees, even in the marketplace's "carrot and stick" world. The study indicated that subordinates whose managers best met the needs for competence, relatedness, and autonomy outperformed others and experienced lower levels of stress. Earlier studies also linked this motivational condition to greater longevity in jobs, with less turnover for the employer.

The principles and practices discussed in previous chapters flow naturally into the leadership of workers. So we will translate each of them below, adding amplification where appropriate.* Then we will take on the tough topic of: "Okay,

---

*Because we are now turning our attention to employees who work largely to earn a living (an extrinsic reason), we note the following. When employees are given sufficient control over how a job gets done—being "empowered" in contemporary managerial jargon—the motivational experience contains many elements associated with intrinsic self-motivation. The experience and consequences of what researchers call self-regulated extrinsic motivation very much approximate intrinsic motivation, so we will continue to use this latter term, having noted the distinction.

but what if my attempts to foster intrinsic motivation aren't working?" (If you have an employee with whom you are having a particularly difficult time and you dread even dealing with that person about job performance, see the next chapter.)

Motivational Lessons from "A Brand New Car Company"

We begin this discussion by sharing a few insights gleaned from analyses of a recent American success story: the Saturn Corporation of General Motors. This new unit incorporated some novel ideas when it established itself in the late 1980s (Gwynne 1990). While not perfect, the approach this company used resulted in a highly successful product, with an unusually motivated workforce. We hope that examining how this inspired management addressed each of the innate needs (competence, relatedness, autonomy) will stimulate your own creative applications in your church (Baard in press).

Competence

Competence involves growing and experiencing challenges to one's current abilities or knowledge. This does not necessarily entail exciting new things to do each workday. Much of one's work, whether it is building a house, maintaining a home, teaching a class, or seeing patients entails routine chores and tasks. The competence need expresses itself in a desire to have *some* growth experience over a reasonable period of time.

Saturn Motors Corporation built such possibilities into its *procedures*. All employees would spend 5 percent of their time in training. This was an intriguing proposition for UAW members accustomed to physically demanding labor throughout their forty-hour work week. Training to do one's specific job could be expected, but then what? Becoming acquainted with other functions along the assembly line would be a natural

Leadership Behaviors That Support Competence

1. Train, prepare, and support subordinates to maximize their probability of success.
2. Remove barriers to efficient performance including physical (for example, air quality) and procedural (for example, unnecessary rules).
3. Agree on achievable goals that are discussed with employees rather than imposed upon them.
4. Help determine reasonable ambitions to improve the probability of subordinates' career successes.
5. Provide optimal challenges by delegating interesting assignments and tasks that develop new skills.
6. Ensure that feedback occurs regularly so that timely corrections can be made.
7. Keep critical comments in perspective, not offering too much negative feedback at once.
8. Encourage self-discovery of errors, allowing workers time to address them on their own whenever possible.

---

progression. Yet all of that would take only a few months at an average of two hours per week. What then? Saturn had in mind teaching its employees practical life skills, completely unrelated to building good cars. These workers would be kept growing throughout their careers, an intrinsic need being met by employer Saturn.

Providing workers with the very best equipment was another Saturn policy that clearly addressed the competence need. In addition, putting fewer work rules in place enabled the assembly-line workers to obtain their own replacement tools without submitting a request to a remote center, thus eliminating the frustration of waiting for the item to be delivered. The company also entrusted each work unit with the power to choose its own suppliers, even of significant components of the vehicles it was assembling. Changes such as these augmented worker satisfaction and enabled more work to be accomplished in a creative fashion.

Regardless of organizational policies or procedures, supervisors and managers can often address the need for competence on a day-to-day basis. Examples include giving a receptionist, usually charged only with greeting visitors and performing light clerical tasks, the responsibility for arranging production of photo identification tags for new employees. While not necessarily a challenging assignment to many, this task makes the receptionist more valuable to the company and could provide a sense of greater competence. At a higher organizational level, allowing middle-level executives the opportunity to develop a draft of the business plan for their work unit is another example of growth enhancement. Some frequently occurring opportunities for those in supervisory positions to support the competence need in their subordinates appear in the listing on p. 86.

Relatedness

Experiencing mutual reliance and respect is at the heart of relatedness. It is about feeling connected, sharing a mutual goal, and being in a relationship for the long haul. The downsizing that persists in corporate America is an obvious threat to satisfying this innate need. And though not even a company's chief executive officer can say with absolute assurance there will be no future layoffs, managers can endeavor to express care for employees when a downsizing occurs (Brockner 1992).

Organizational procedures provide an institutional opportunity to support the need for relatedness. Saturn Motors

Leadership Behaviors That Support Relatedness

1. Hold regular meetings so you are easily accessible even to those who are somewhat timid about coming to your office.
2. Set reward structures that support cooperation and diminish competition between individuals or teams.
3. Avoid triangulation, that is, turning to a third party when frustrated by the performance of an employee who is not present.
4. Share information whenever feasible, trusting your associates to keep certain matters confidential.
5. Conduct team-building exercises when appropriate. (Note: Such efforts need not be dramatic, such as wilderness excursions, to be effective. A friendly but competitive game allows participants the opportunity to see some office behaviors under a different light.)

Corporation built in some ideas that were not only novel but also provocative to the automotive industry at the time (O'Toole 1996). Each work unit would be responsible for hiring its own members. Since a new culture of quality and efficient work was to be a core value of Saturn, on-line workers interviewed and selected new members of their team with those standards in mind. In this way the team was able to communicate its insistence upon a new attitude toward work. Calling in sick on Mondays would be challenged by one's peers. And since group members selected future co-workers, peer acceptance and support began immediately for the new hire.

Introducing job rotation, with members of work units changing roles every so often, created greater empathy and respect for a colleague's work. In addition, the heads of labor and of management had offices immediately adjacent to one another, visually and practicably lessening a "them vs. us" orientation, while promoting a natural sharing of information. Their daily exchanges communicated a "togetherness" to the organization (O'Toole 1996).

Looking at the larger workplace, even if divisive organizational practices such as internally competitive bonus systems undermine a manager's attempt at "team building," daily interactive opportunities still afford the insightful manager a chance to satisfy the relatedness needs of subordinates. The listing on p. 88 indicates some of these opportunities.

Autonomy

Autonomy involves sensing some level of control and choice about the work one is doing. It is not about managers being permissive or neglectful, but rather about subordinates having influence in the workplace. "Empowerment" is the management term often used to connote this notion of shared responsibility in how work gets done.

Several practices at Saturn were directed at worker autonomy. Because it would be a unionized work force (as is true for production-line workers throughout General Motors), Saturn wanted to staff the company with current employees wishing to join in the building of "a different kind of car" by a "different kind of company" (O'Toole 1996). The new Saturn plant would be in Spring Hill, Tennessee, far from the assembly lines and corporate culture of Detroit-area facilities. The initial staffing would consist of UAW volunteers who would leave their established places of work and the advantages of their earned seniority to participate in this new venture. An individual's decision even to work at this new plant, therefore, was an entirely autonomous one.

Saturn took a second autonomy-supportive step by includ-

Leadership Behaviors That Support Autonomy

1. Optimize subordinates' control and influence over how their work gets done, bonuses are structured, goals are set, etc.
2. Ameliorate internal and external pressures rather than simply passing them on.
3. Reduce or eliminate excessive rules, making certain that outdated organizational policies do not impede performance.
4. Allow self-selection for tasks whenever possible.
5. Permit failure when feasible (the inability to fail implies rigid boundaries of behavior).
6. Take the subordinate's perspective, at least initially (even if you believe it to be inaccurate), before you try to explain your view of the situation.
7. Provide feedback in a noncontrolling manner so your subordinate does not feel pressured into a position.
8. Choose an assertive communication style rather than using controlling (aggressive) language, for example, "I believe you would benefit from..." vs. "You should...."
9. Avoid manipulative incentive systems by using rewards as affirmation of work done well rather than a means to get more out of an employee.

---

ing the workers in nearly all decisions, from how a bonus system would work to which advertising agency would handle the car's introductory promotion campaign. This inclusiveness was most unusual in the often antagonistic "labor vs. management" world of auto manufacturing in the United States (O'Toole 1996).

Perhaps the most significant support for autonomy, however, was a very subtle one. At each workstation along the assembly line hung a cord with a blue handle at its end, above head level but within reach. Every worker was empowered to pull that cord and stop the entire production line if he or she detected a systemic problem. For example, if someone assigned to the tire-mounting unit noted something misaligned, that worker normally would tag the car and a correction would be made at some point down the line. However, if a Saturn worker saw the next car with the same problem, that worker could stop production. This is a significant responsibility for line workers, many of whom have limited education and have never been given this level of authority in their careers. While the need to pull the lever is rare, it is the knowledge that they *could* do so that supports a sense of autonomy. Any managerial fears that UAW members would misuse this power were dispelled as workers responsibly handled this delegation of authority.

While there are many organizational means for either supporting or frustrating the need for autonomy, the research suggests that day-to-day experiences with one's immediate supervisor can help ameliorate even a relatively controlling atmosphere (Baard, Deci, and Ryan 1999). The listing on p. 90 identifies some of these means.

While managing a church is quite different from overseeing a production line, people are people. In fact, motivationally speaking, churches probably have a better opportunity for intrinsic motivation in the employment venue because the "product" we turn out—the opportunity for people to draw closer to God—is surely superior to even the noble task of turning out a good automobile!

Besides, we had better have a maximal level of intrinsic motivation going for us: our wages do not compare favorably to those of the United Auto Workers.

But What about My Helpless Handyman and Rueful Receptionist?

Sometimes we encounter "problem employees." Let us first state emphatically: resist labeling anyone (as we just did!). Doing so has two undesirable effects: it tends to exaggerate the problem, and it makes the problem seem to be a negative character trait rather than an issue of behavior, which is correctable. So let's refer to these individuals as "employees with a problem."

In this kind of a situation, where someone is performing poorly either because of laziness or carelessness, we can identify the problem in motivational terms. The individual is in an amotivated state. Our goal in intervening, indicated in figure 4, is to move the person along the motivational continuum from amotivation (AM) through extrinsic motivation (EM), with the eventual hope of igniting intrinsic motivation (IM).

Figure 4. The Motivational Continuum

IM .... EM .... AM

IM = Intrinsic Motivation
EM = Extrinsic Motivation
AM = Amotivation

To speak to employees who are not getting the job done in terms of delighting in their work (which would necessitate a direct movement from amotivation to intrinsic motivation) would leave us sounding as if we had recently arrived from Mars. So, instead, a carrot-and-sticking we will go!

Reinforcement Theory

Reinforcement theory, often identified with behavior modification, uses principles derived from the pioneering work of theorists such as B. F. Skinner, who focused his work on studying the conditions that bring about change by modifying the environment surrounding his subjects (which were often pigeons or mice). His was the stuff of extrinsic—"What's in it for me?"—motivation. (Skinner's work was so effective that many schools, unfortunately, used his findings to model and develop educational practices. As a result, many children now delight more in getting a gold star than in discovery and mastery.) While this type of drive in the workplace is not as effective in most respects as that produced by intrinsic motivation, it is a step up from amotivation: "How little do I have to do and not be fired?"

There are a number of principles we can derive from reinforcement theory. The effort, however, all begins with confronting the employee. Remarkably, many a church leader tolerates increasingly poor performance without ever directly addressing the matter. Late arrival, for example, is ignored because "Well, he's basically doing the job, and I don't want to stir up a discussion that could lead to complaints about his wage level or work responsibilities." Performance gaps are downplayed because "sometimes it's better to let these things correct themselves." Experience has shown, however, that they seldom turn for the better, and they carry a "spread-of-effect" to others.

Behavioral Modification Techniques

It is important to keep in mind several caveats. If, for example, your position does not encompass the authority to see this process to its conclusion, which may mean the individual's termination, then it is best to proceed only if the person who does have the authority is willing to stand by your decisions. At every step of the process, it is essential to keep a written record of what transpired, that is, times, dates, and descriptions of the conversations you have had with the employee. Finally, if your vision of church employer-employee work relations does not allow you to hold a paid employee accountable, then you have no need to continue with the rest of this chapter. Unfortunately, there are many church leaders who do not think it possible to terminate a person in their employ. Often this comes from a misguided sense of Christian love and responsibility. Experience has shown, however, that allowing employees to continue performing poorly can destroy staff morale and at the same time hamper the congregation's attempt to serve others, both in and outside of the church.

The techniques of behavior modification listed below should be applied *sequentially,* as presented.

Step 1: Articulate Expectations Clearly

This is not the time for subtle, read-between-the-lines communication. Mentioning to a nearby employee that you really appreciate how thorough she is in performing her duties—in a voice loud enough for Gus to hear and hopefully to heed—is ineffective most of the time. Likewise, mentioning Gus's poor performance to his co-workers in the hope that the message will get back to him "through the grapevine" is also an inappropriate way to deal with the situation.

Your clear, assertive discussion might better go like this: "Gus, I really appreciate the work you are doing around here. The church and rectory are in good condition. Because [notice we didn't use "but," which negates everything in the communication up to that point] we have so many people in and out of here all the time, it's important to always have things neat and orderly. It presents an inviting atmosphere. Please take care to leave the work area spotless so our people see the respect we have for *their* house of worship."

As for the habitually late-arriving receptionist: "Roberta,

we have had many compliments about your efficiency in handling requests from members. Thank you for meeting those needs so well. It is important also for you to be here promptly at 9:00 A.M. That's when the calls start coming in and members sometimes stop by. Please take care to arrive promptly in the future." Merely bringing a deficiency to an individual's attention is often sufficient to correct the problem.

In dealing with these problems, it will serve a leader well to turn to the Spirit for guidance. If, however, the employee, confronted with his work deficiency, asks to pray with his or her boss, the matter becomes delicate. A shared prayer can be mistaken for a shared responsibility for the problem. We advise an initial prayer, if requested. After that, however, the manager should encourage the employee to search out a colleague or prayer group, in order to keep the lines of accountability clear.

Step 2: Look For and Reward Partial Improvement

The track we are on is called successive approximation. A natural tendency, of course, is to think, "Employees should just get it done!" That, say psychologists, is the neurotic world of "should," the way life ought to be—and isn't. Scientists have discovered the most efficient way to bring about change: incrementally. So we look for some noticeable improvement in the targeted behavior. We discover Gus clearing up at least most of the mess, or Roberta arriving only five minutes late instead of ten.

We reward that partial gain by using a *positive reinforcer,* that is, anything that brings about what we are after in that individual. Is a compliment a positive reinforcer? Yes, but only if it works for *that person* regarding *that behavior.* Some people respond well to a word of appreciation; others do not. Some to a cup of tea; others to a gesture of assistance. This approach works far more effectively than the traditional managerial tool, namely, punishments, such as reprimands and warnings. While sometimes punishments are necessary, as we soon shall see they are simply less efficient in bringing about change.

Of course, you have to know the person to determine what will serve as a positive reinforcer. When you see a slight improvement, reinforce it only once. Remember, you are out to correct the whole problem. When even further gains are noted, reinforce again. As to the possible concern that others who are doing their jobs correctly might object to your affirming Gus's improvement, hopefully you have been reinforcing their behavior all along.

And what if there is no improvement, initially or ongoing?

Step 3: Start to Use Negative Reinforcers

The next most efficient means for bringing about behavioral change is to introduce something *continuously* irritating to the individual, for example, nagging. Ask the mother of any teenager: "Did you clean up your room yet?" will soon be followed by "Did you clean up your room yet?" And on it will go. The only way for junior to stop this irritating line of inquiry is to—you've already guessed.

The intent is to present a state of affairs that remains unpleasant until the targeted behavior has been addressed. For example, if the desired outcome is the removal of clutter from an office, a manager might *constantly* bring this need to the subordinate's attention until it is addressed. In the early part of the day the manager might inquire, "Gus, have you finished cleaning the room yet?" Later in the morning the manager repeats, "I really need that room cleaned for a meeting later this evening. Please report to me when you complete it so I can set the room up properly." Later in the afternoon, if the task remains undone, the leader can check on Gus's progress: "Gus,

I am at a standstill until the room is cleaned. I need you to complete this so I can prepare for my meeting."

One caution: this deliberately irritating technique can lead to "numbing," as we readily observe in the teenager with the messy room. It also can increase the manager's level of stress. Note also that the time frame one uses for this technique depends upon the individual manager. Some find negative reinforcers difficult to employ even for short periods of time; others can go on indefinitely. Regardless of your own personal style, however, having a definite time frame in mind is helpful so you don't remain—forever frustrated—at step three. Often one must move to step four.

Step 4: Explain Potential Consequences of Continued Poor Performance

For many Christian leaders, the thought of confronting an individual causes considerable discomfort. After all, are not Christians called to forgive? Such a stance comes from an incorrect notion of Christian forgiveness and love, as well as a failure to separate the person from the behavior. Behavioral modification strives to modify the behavior, not devalue the individual. Explaining the potential consequences of continued poor performance addresses the person's behavior; it does not denigrate the person. In fact, it is a very caring thing to do since it improves the employee's probability of success.

Church leaders may fear that the employee will either quit or make an end run to someone in higher authority or to one who could make life difficult for them. The exchange might even cause dissension within the church itself. All these fears are understandable. It is important, therefore, to recognize them, name them, and take control over them so they do not control you.

This fact is undeniable: leaders who are unwilling to lose

a particular employee for whatever reason are thereby stuck with that employee, regardless of the individual's behavior. In effect, that employee now manages the church leader. Often our insecure thinking paralyzes us from moving directly on these matters. The next chapter will address this issue.

To confront the matter at hand, first speak with the employee in a private setting in order not to embarrass him or her in front of others. Make clear that things must change: "Gus, I have spoken to you about the need for after-job cleanup. Things are not improving. This is a requirement of the job, for the reasons I have explained. If the matter is not corrected over the next two weeks, I will be unable to continue extending this job opportunity to you. Please take care of this. I really want you here on the church team." Note there was no mention of shared responsibility here, that is, "Is there a problem with things here? Is there anything I can do to help?" While this sounds very caring, and indeed people expect a manager or supervisor in a church setting to hold to the "Servant Leader" model, such questions send a mixed message. The opportunity to deal with the possibility that Gus may have had a "problem with things" or needed something to do his job correctly was back at step one when articulating expectations. Leaders who bring this up now run the risk of being accountable to Gus for doing their managerial job satisfactorily!

If the attempts described above have worked and the behavior has now been corrected, be sure to reinforce the improvement. Express appreciation, and note the progress during the annual performance review. (If you do not have an annual review, please refer to chapter 3 on competence and the need for feedback. In addition, appendix 3 (p. 127) offers performance appraisal guidelines, while Baard and Neville 1996 provide additional ideas pertaining to employee evaluation and feedback sessions.) Examples of long-term reinforcers include adding desirable work responsibilities and providing better equipment.

Okay, but what if things *still* haven't improved?

Step 5: Punish, with Termination of Employment as the Final Action

According to social scientists, reaching for this final tool of behavioral modification is using the least effective method of bringing about enduring change (Hamner 1974). In some instances, of course, punishment is ultimately necessary and effective. There are, however, some negative aspects of this step. Punishment evokes strong emotional reactions about fairness and detracts from the relearning process. It sometimes sends employees to their colleagues for reassurance that the leader really is an unappreciative, rotten boss.

And yet, if all else has failed, punishment may be the only tool remaining, short of termination. The best way to administer punishment, of course, is to have it "fit the crime." If lateness persists, you may have to dock the receptionist's pay. If the room is not cleaned, you may have to require the custodian to remain after hours without monetary compensation. Obviously, we know whether the punishment is effective only if it changes the targeted behavior. When using this tool, it is essential that the leader has apprised the employee of the situation and its consequences and has kept written documentation.

Finally, the situation may require the termination of employment. No one, of course, wishes a situation to come to this conclusion. It is "no-win" from every point of view. Unfortunately, it is sometimes necessary for the well-being of the church community and for the future growth of the employee. (At this point, it may be helpful to review the introductory remarks under "Behavioral Modification Techniques" concerning adequate top leadership support; see above p. 93.)

When termination of employment becomes necessary, it should be handled with dignity. You should express regret for how things have turned out and wish the very best for the ex-employee. This is not the time to rehash things. If it can be arranged for the person to resign, so much the better with respect for his or her work record, let alone any legal consequences. Financial matters will need to be considered, for example, back pay, accumulated vacation days, and unemployment compensation. Consult your church's accountant or a human resources specialist, if there is one in your congregation, to make sure that these matters are handled properly.

Will Behavioral Modification Work?

Many good leaders intuitively employ the techniques of behavior modification in their day-to-day dealings. In fact, the popular book *The One Minute Manager* book is based upon some of these principles (Blanchard and Johnson 1982). However, this approach is best used only when an attempt to tap into an employee's intrinsic motivation is proving unproductive. Again, the goal is to cause movement from amotivation to extrinsic motivation. When this shift occurs, a leader can usually count on the work environment to reinforce the new productive behaviors. Fellow employees usually know what is going on and encourage the recovering employee.

If even the thought of addressing such problematic situations leaves you feeling anxious, we invite you to the next chapter.

Chapter Seven

Psychological Fusion
When Other People Can "Make Us Feel"

Make every effort to live in peace with all.
—Hebrews 12:14 NIV

"Sure, these motivational improvements can be made in a *normal* church, but not when you have to deal with Deacon Dan, as we must!"

Sometimes people resist change as if their very lives were somehow endangered by the move. The emotionality displayed in such resistance just doesn't seem to fit. It appears out of proportion to the substance of the proposed change. "We are just trying to improve the efficiency of the budgeting process by working with you to create a computer data base for contributions," the wearied pastor explains, yet again, to Dan, who has been the church treasurer for the past twenty-two years. Dan can come up with a hundred reasons why a new system won't work or is not needed. "My green ledger books work fine," he asserts. As perplexing as we might find Dan's response, equally perplexing is the pastor's toleration of that response, as he allows Dan's obstructionism to continue.

This phenomenon, called "psychological fusion" by Paul P. Baard, occurs *when the actions of others are interpreted as a threat to one's sense of self-worth* (see Baard 1994c for an illustration of how psychological fusion can undermine the functioning of a group). Psychological fusion involves that curious dynamic which occurs when our mere perception of the intent of others (what we think they *really* meant by what they said or did) can actually bring about an emotional response in us. It is as if we were momentarily connected at the brain with the other, as if the other's thoughts, or at least our perception of them, could actually cause anxiety. We all know that our brain's functioning can affect our nervous systems. By worrying constantly for a prolonged period, we can develop ulcers or heart disease. But that another person's thinking, or at least our inference of it, can cause an emotional response in us is worth examining.

The dynamic of psychological fusion is behind such familiar everyday phenomena as road rage. Think, for example, what occurs when a driver cuts in front of us. At first we're momentarily startled. But then we take one of two paths. We can take the "high road" by calming down, viewing the encounter as a reflection of the other driver's rudeness or carelessness, concluding that the driver was either inconsiderate or clumsy, and being thankful we have escaped harm. Or we might take the "low road" by becoming angry: "Who does he think he is doing that to me!" In this case we actually have a sense of having been demeaned. This path often ignites within us a desire for revenge or retaliation, which we might then act out with angry words, gestures, or aggressive driving. Our behavior may evoke a similar response in the other driver, and on it goes. Or one may simply contain one's rage, imploding instead of exploding, and carry the rage into another situation, "letting it loose" against a spouse, child, or friend over whom there is a better chance of coming out on top.

Most emotional overreaction comes about because we experience offensive behavior as a put-down, an insult, a slighting of ourselves. The provocation can be as subtle as an unreturned "Good morning," making us think "Who does she think she is!" We feel somehow demeaned, and we don't like the feeling at all. And if a significant other is present, our emotional pain and subsequent anger are intensified as we are embarrassed or even ashamed.

The degree to which we derive a *disproportionate* amount of our self-regard or self-worth from a particular job or position indicates the degree to which we have become fused to that job or position. In effect, we *need* that job in order to be fully ourselves. While it is true that most of us need *a* job, in truth, we don't need *that* job. This is quite different from wanting the position because we derive enjoyment from it. In the example of Deacon Dan, his position as church deacon and treasurer constituted his very self-identity in an unhealthy and disproportionate way. In other words, he had allowed his self-worth to become fused with his position as deacon and job as treasurer.

Not long ago in the corporate world, there lived a breed of employee called "lifers." These were men and women who had chosen to spend most of their careers with one company, for example, IBM ("Big Blue") or other such prominent corporations. That may have been consistent with notions of corporate loyalty some business leaders liked to nurture, but when layoffs began at these corporate giants in the 1990s, there were many senior employees who suffered a sense of loss of personal identity when they were encouraged to leave. Those individuals had become psychologically fused to being IBMers or GMers. They had derived too much of their self-identity and self-worth from association with a prestigious firm, rather than properly valuing themselves as parents, spouses, children of God, citizens, church members, and all their other valuable roles.

Conflict at Church

Despite the scriptural admonition to "live in peace with all," we fall short here as we do almost everywhere. Some harbor grudges over perceived or real slights; others resist doing the better thing, preferring to stay in a comfort zone rather than making needed improvements in their ministries (Baard 1998). Still others use emotional bullying to impose their wills on groups. There are personality conflicts with some; others have oversensitive reactions to anything that might be interpreted as critical feedback. Some engage in triangulation, in which a person feeling anxious about another turns to a third party in the hope of gaining an ally to agree that the other is at fault. More than likely, such modes of relating are not foreign to your church community. You've undoubtedly experienced first hand the damage they can cause, literally strangling any sense of trust and family in a congregation. Even those in the highest levels of leadership are not exempt from these human failings. We all have our insecurities. To explore ways to ameliorate these day-to-day people problems, we will examine a leading theory in clinical psychology, Bowen Family Systems Theory, and its concept of differentiation of self.

Behind the Conflict: Differentiation of Self

Bowen Family Systems Theory (Kerr and Bowen 1988) articulates a concept called differentiation of self which is, essentially, emotional maturation. For discussion purposes, Bowen devised a hypothetical, nonempirical scale of 0–100 to describe the emotional development of individuals, beginning at birth (see figure 5). He conceptualizes the neonate as having no real sense of self—of being an individual distinct from all others. The infant's life is all about needing and feeling; parental approval, expressed as cooing, gentle speech,

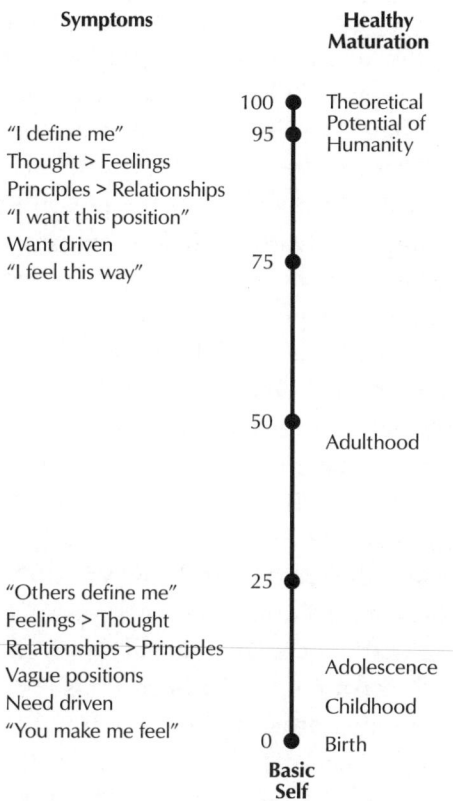

Figure 5. Bowen's Scale of Differentiation

and physical gestures, results in a happy, contented baby. A disapproving frown, however, leads to a frightened child, who will likely cry or become tense. There isn't much thinking going on in those early days; the infant's behavior is dictated by emotions triggered entirely by others.

With time, however, children begin to differentiate themselves, gaining some level of control over their responses.

They get a sense of what they are good at, and not so good at. In a healthy family, parents facilitate this process by starting to emphasize a child's distinctiveness, rather than simply affirming the fact that the child belongs to that family. Where once it was "Oh, you have a beautiful smile, just like Mom's," Dad's words gradually start to acknowledge differentness. Picture the junior high student coming home from a social studies lecture about the positive aspects of socialist governments. "Dad, I think socialism is better than capitalism because in those countries everybody gets health care even if they are poor." In an open-systems family—open in the sense of allowing differentness to occur—Dad's response might sound something like: "Well, Honey, you're able to go to that terrific school because of capitalism, but the truth is, you make an interesting point. Let's discuss that tonight at the dinner table." Dad has taken this opportunity to affirm his daughter's individuality—that it's okay to think thoughts that are different from Mom's and Dad's.

In a closed-systems family, however, distinctiveness is discouraged. "Is that where all the unemployed commies are working now? In our school system?" is a facetious illustration of a family intolerant of diverse thinking. "We're capitalists here!" the offspring is reminded. In effect, the child has been told, "If you want to fit in around here, to be accepted, you must think the way we do." The ultimate product of such a household is an emotionally undifferentiated adult, one who continues to depend upon parental approval—and by extension, the approval of others—for a sense of self-worth. Such emotionally fused individuals must be hypervigilant concerning their environment since their sense of well-being rises on a compliment and falls on a criticism. They *need* other people's acceptance and will compromise their principles to obtain this acceptance. For such persons, *feelings* are the deciding factor in dictating behavior. Well-differentiated individuals, however, while wanting acceptance by others, will not compromise their principles to obtain acceptance in relationships. *Thought* predominates in their behavioral response, although feelings are indeed taken into account.

Bowen saw humanity as largely clustered in the 25–75 range. Those at the higher levels appear emotionally more stable, able to take strong stands on principle, and are less vulnerable to emotional overreactions to perceived slights. Adults in the "under 25" range, however, are often conspicuously dysfunctional in society. Bowen further asserted that the 95–100 range represented humanity's potential, that is, people who would not compromise principles for the sake of relationships, yet would die for another. This certainly is an apt description of our Lord, who did not compromise a single principle for the sake of being accepted, yet willingly laid down his life for all.

In summary, Bowen's concept of differentiation of self addresses the growth process in which we gain control over our emotions. In young children, feelings drive their response to situations. In emotionally mature adults, while feelings play a role in their responses, thoughts and principles are the primary guides. They define self and do not depend upon others to do so. This contrasts with persons who are primarily reactive: a compliment in the morning can make their day, and a criticism can break it. Such vulnerable individuals must be hypervigilant all day long, constantly on the lookout for evaluative input—real or imagined—from the environment.

The Trigger of the Conflict: Psychological Fusion

The concept of psychological fusion, derived from Bowen Systems Theory (Baard 1994b), describes the response that an event in our environment triggers when experienced as a threat to our personhood. It is termed "psychological" because it is a trick of the mind; it is "fusion" because what we think the person was thinking caused us to feel, as if our brains were momentarily joined.

For example, a colleague might offer a gratuitous criticism. In its mildest form, we have a startled response: our attention is heightened. We then choose either to respond to, or to ignore, the negative stimulus. Upon quick reflection—knowing the individual—we might discern this to be a bit of jealousy extended toward us. Choosing to treat it as such, we do not respond: "not a big deal." Or we may choose to express our surprise at the evaluative comment and inquire about its purpose or meaning. Note the word "choose": we can either choose not to respond, or to respond with our feelings and thoughts under control. Another possibility, of course, is that we find ourselves reacting almost involuntarily to the critical remark. In such a case our "response" is based on emotional compulsion, that is, an automated, fused response. We might feel compelled to even the score and counterattack with a negative, sarcastic comment. Or we might remain silent for fear of losing an argument with this aggressor. (Note that an automated, fused response need not involve an outward display of disproportionate emotion.) Regardless, the other individual's comment "caused" us to respond.

In the first scenario, where the person was actually choosing how to strategically and purposefully respond, there was evidence of adequate individuation, an indication of someone higher up on the Bowen scale of differentiation of self. In the second scenario, the person lost all sense of choosing, falling into a reactive stance fueled by emotion. Such a person might be found lower on the Bowen scale.

Of course, any one of us can have a fused response to a stimulus. After a particularly demanding day at our job we might be sharing a significant success with our spouse. All it takes, if we are sufficiently tired or stressed, is a stifled yawn by our partner to trigger an emotional overreaction: "That's how little you care about me?!" Under normal circumstances, however, the likelihood of a psychologically fused response correlates with a person's emotional maturation or differentiation of self. We are most vulnerable to fusing, that is, allowing the perceived opinions of others to evoke a response in us, when we are not adequately self-defined in a given area. Tips on ameliorating this inadequacy appear later in the chapter.

We can measure the degree of the propensity a person has toward psychological fusion, and hence get an indication of that person's emotional differentiation of self, by using two variables. First, there is the *intensity* of the triggered emotional response, including acting-out behavior as well as internal anguish. The second variable is the amount of *time* it takes that person to return to a state of emotional normalcy, or acting like his or her true self (see figure 6 on the following page). In terms of the intensity variable, someone low on the differentiation of self scale can be expected to go to an extreme in either of two directions. One would be a very energized implosion in which the person worries intensely about the possible outcome of an exchange and moves to placate the other, seeking assurance or forgiveness, regardless of actually accepting responsibility for a conflict. The other extreme would be an explosion, for example, cursing, threatening, or stomping out of the room. In terms of the time variable, the co-worker or neighbor who stays angry for years over a perceived slight would appear to be low on the scale of emotional differentiation. These dynamics are illustrated in figure 6.

Note that the departure from "true self" (who we genuinely are, represented by the vertical line on Bowen's scale of differentiation) is depicted along the broken horizontal line. If we "travel" to the left, we depart from what we truly stand for

Figure 6. The Degree of Psychological Fusion

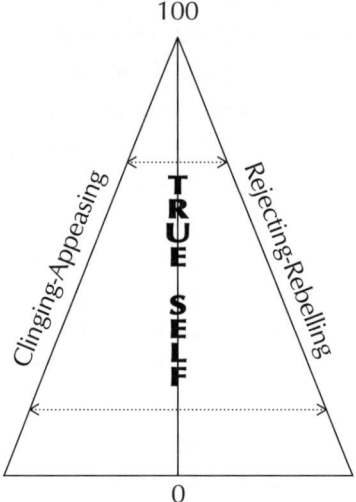

and are ready to do anything to retain the relationship: "I'll do anything to keep my job!" is the tone. Or, if we move to the right, we are attempting to reject the other: "They are all a bunch of idiots around here, anyway. Who needs them!" Both of these responses—placating or rebelling—are two sides of the same coin. Take, for example, the spurned suitor. He might approach his target with all sorts of promises to change, to reform, to be "anything you want me to be." Hearing "No, it's not going to happen," he might then respond with a threat: "If I can't have you, no one will!" In both extreme scenarios, the person evinces a dramatic departure from being a genuine person, as he readily will compromise personal principles for the sake of that relationship. A healthy, proportionate response in the situation might be an appeal to the former companion along these lines: "I now realize how wrong I was in my conduct. I am going to seek help. I hope you take me back, but I will address this concern nonetheless." The rejected one demonstrates that he wants the other, but does not need her to be his authentic self.

One critical variable in these responses is the level of anxiety we experience. Anxiety releases chemicals in the brain directly affecting emotions. The "fight or flight" response ensues from a startled reaction. The chemicals flood out of the frontal lobes in the brain, impairing rational thought. Raw emotion, not reasoned choice, then dictates response. Obviously when we feel our personhood is tied into being, for example, "chairman of the Board of Deacons," any dissenting comments by fellow deacons are potentially psychologically life-threatening. And so an intense response, disproportionate to the matter at hand, can be expected.

Ameliorating Psychological Conflict

Clearly the best route to reducing the effects of psychological fusion is to progress along the emotional maturation scale. This is done by clearly defining oneself—acknowledging our strengths and accepting our weaknesses—and liking ourselves. It is, of course, biblical: Love your neighbor as yourself" (Mark 12:31). Most psychologists will agree that this acceptance is key to emotional health. We are not talking of a haughty or narcissistic posture: those who genuinely embark on this task will be humbled by the deficiencies they identify. Once we have done this, when another points out a fault in us, it is non-news; we are free from emotional reactivity and able to analyze the speaker's intent. If someone flatters us, we are able to better discern the flatterer's motivation, leaving us less susceptible to emotional manipulation.

There will be times, however, when an unexpected criticism

Figure 7. The Process of Psychologically Fused and Unfused Responding

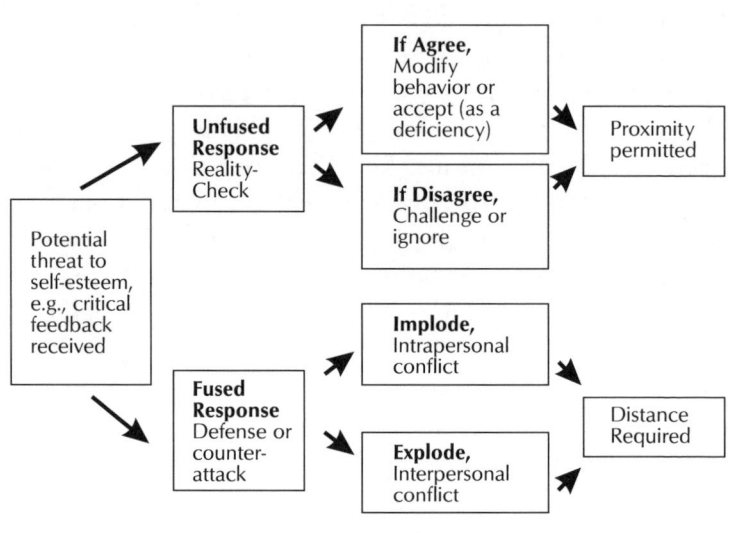

can startle us: after all, few of us truly delight in rejection. Here is where our thinking skills can continue to control our response. Figure 7 depicts two response paths: the "high road" shows how we might think following receipt of a criticism, let us say, from a boss.

The first step is a reality check: Is the observation accurate? If we agree, for example, with our manager's assessment that our time management skills need improving, we might decide to take a time management course. Or perhaps we have so much on our plate at the moment, for example, a new baby at home or the conclusion of an advanced degree at night, that the addition of one more initiative could be the straw that breaks us. In this case we might simply accept a lower evaluation in that category, for the time being. Or we might feel the assessment is unfair. For example, we might be the member of the work unit taking on the most work and now find ourselves faulted for being slower than the others in submitting our weekly activity report. And so we might take it upon ourselves to point out, assertively and respectfully, this inequity. Unfortunately, the response is sometimes immediate and reactive: "Well," the fused manager might retort, feeling his authority challenged, "I had rated you highly in the 'Able to accept criticism' category, but I now see I should lower your rating in that area." During future performance reviews, the subordinate might choose to ignore this manager's occasionally inaccurate assessments, since he is obviously too weak a manager to correct a mistake. An important point to note is that responses governed by thinking rather than emotional reaction preserve proximity to the other. That is to say, we can continue in a functioning relationship with the other person since that individual is not capable of causing us serious emotional pain.

Now let us examine "the low road" of psychologically fused response. Perceiving a criticism as an attack on our self-worth rather than an assessment of certain things we do, we move to protect ourselves through a defense or counterattack. When dealing with a boss, if we fear possible reprisal should we speak out, we might implode. Outwardly we say things like: "Well, I realize it is your job to point out areas where workers are deficient, and I appreciate your doing so. I'll get right on it and improve for next time." Inside, we are deeply resentful of this attack on our personhood, even going so far as to silently wish our manager ill. Or we might explode, threatening to go over our boss's head to the top manager and countering with criticisms of our own. Either of these two responses virtually precludes a future relationship. This person has the ability to hurt us emotionally, and we want to avoid him or her.

Psychological fusion often accounts for the organizational paralysis readily observed in workplaces of all sorts. Deacon Dan fights to maintain the status quo, while the pastor fears offending Dan and his block of supporters. Nothing is getting done, as the pastor frets away the opportunity to take necessary initiatives for growth. The key here is to act unilaterally: decisively, yet respectfully. The pastor, for example, can approach Dan with empathy. "I can understand your hesitation to embrace this change. You have guided this church well in the matter of financial accountability to our congregation. In order for us to take full advantage of new investment strategies, however, we need a more timely and flexible way to anticipate cash flow. Rest assured, we want you overseeing this project. But it must be done, and done promptly. Will you stand with us?" In most cases, given the alternative of take it or let go of it, the Dans of our world will acquiesce. And if not, we must be prepared to accept an occasional resignation. Obviously, these measures are not taken lightly, and at times there will be fallout. Tolerating such noncooperation, however, brings about a great deal of discord, some of which is not readily apparent. Seeing the lack of decisive action by a leader, the people who could contribute significantly may opt to stay on the sidelines, not wishing to waste their time in a poorly led effort.

Introducing Change

The motivational leader understands how change inherently contains the capacity to deliver intrinsic motivation. The challenge of introducing a new way of doing things carries with it a growth opportunity (satisfying the need for competence). It almost always entails a real team effort to accomplish it (satisfying the need for relatedness). And competent leaders will take steps to involve everyone in how the change is brought about (satisfying the need for autonomy).

Understanding how psychological fusion functions in organizations helps a leader address the root causes of resistance. The threats that some perceive with respect to change may entail a simple fear of failure. They may think that their current skill or knowledge level is insufficient to do the job. The obvious approach is to provide help, either by personal assistance or outside support. For example, you might pay to have the individual attend a relevant course offered at a local school or professional agency, or hire a consultant to provide in-house training. Sometimes people fear losing the respect of their peers or church family ("They are finally getting Deacon Dan out of the nineteenth century!"). By having such a person take a public role in describing the planned changes at church, that person is able to save face.

A leader must be frank with resisters, letting them know that the change is needed and that the church is going forward, hopefully with their full participation (implicitly communicating "...but going forward nonetheless"). Similarly, a commitment to support those currently in the affected roles must be made and kept. Empathy is required, but so is leadership. Not everyone is going to like you, but we suspect you know that all too well already. But by *not* addressing this matter of how psychological fusion sometimes impairs your own leadership effectiveness, growth will be stymied.

In conclusion, psychological fusion describes that all-too-familiar phenomenon in which we find ourselves overreacting to perceived threats in our emotional environment. Fusion often takes the form of clinging to a position as if our very lives depended on it. Although we did not address this explicitly, it can also manifest itself in terms of fusion to an idea or a stance we have taken on an issue. Think of those endless meetings you've attended where someone defends an idea to the death: "That's my baby you're attacking!" Effective church leaders are not averse to helping such individuals realize that it is only an idea out on the table, not themselves. We realize this is easier said than done, but the health of the group depends upon a leader who persists in holding up this reality; otherwise those lacking a healthy sense of self can stymie a group's ability to function (see Baard 1994c).

Acting Unilaterally

In some circumstances, acting in an unfused manner entails proceeding unilaterally. For example, let us say you know that Receptionist Roberta is a bit oversensitive to critical feedback. If you were to delay or minimize needed corrections because of this knowledge, you would be fusing—taking responsibility for her response. You are responsible for *your* end of the transaction, not *hers*. It is most appropriate for you to act empathetically and to speak respectfully by using assertive rather than aggressive speech. "I believe you will find the use of a time organizer book helpful as you handle the increased volume of calls this season" is easier to hear than "You really should use...." Similarly, a feedback session scheduled for Wednesday at 10:00 A.M. could be postponed by the supervisor if she learns that Roberta's grandmother was just rushed to the hospital.

We cannot be held ultimately responsible for the feelings experienced by another. Tempting as it is to believe "you make me so happy," the same person can easily flip that coin to "you make me so miserable." We can only help provide an environment in which people might find delight. The finding is entirely up to them. We may offer ideas to our top leadership and for that we are responsible. Acting on them is up to the recipient. Not to make a suggestion for an improvement we think is needed in the church because "we know they won't implement it," is to perform both sides of the transaction. Some people cease offering their ideas for this reason: psychological fusion has rendered them paralyzed. We must act unilaterally, taking responsibility only for what *we* can do.

Through it all, effective leaders endeavor to get their own fusion under control as they work to have those in their sphere of influence do likewise. Most often it merely takes thoughtful explanations, although employees sometimes need direct professional counseling. Hopefully, your church will seek to provide such resources.

Chapter Eight

The Power of the Spirit

*"Unless the Lord builds the house,
its builders labor in vain."*
—Psalm 127:1 NIV

Intrinsic motivation appears to be part of the design through which the Lord energizes his people to accomplish wonderful things. If your congregation has been enjoying the growth and bounty that comes from the power of the Holy Spirit, praise God. More than likely, however, you are among the majority of church leaders who are experiencing great challenge as you seek church growth in a culture hostile to the Gospel message.

Prayer Is the Key

Intense prayer is both the starting point and a continuing necessity as you endeavor to overcome these challenges and bring about change in your congregation. Through prayer, you are given an ongoing resource for everyday experiences of implementing personal growth, institutional change, and the empowerment of your congregations to live and proclaim the Gospel faithfully. Be certain that God will honor that prayer: "If my people, who are called by my name, will humble themselves and pray and seek my face and turn from their wicked ways, then will I hear from heaven and forgive their sin and will heal their land" (2 Chron. 7:14 NIV).

One author observed a church that was attempting to rebuild a dwindling congregation. They began by designing a new membership campaign that honored different categories of occupations represented throughout the community. There was a Sunday service devoted to elected officials, another to professionals, to teachers, to uniformed services. During the first few weeks, many people came to be honored or to "network" with the honorees. No one, however, returned.

Despite their apparent failure, God used the difficult circumstances in which the congregation found itself to bring the people back to himself. This was done through prayer when the struggling church finally fell to its knees, literally. Realizing they didn't have the answers, many members joined with the leadership in conducting a one-week prayer vigil. From early morning to late each night, someone was in the church sanctuary begging God to forgive the sins of commission as well as omission that had been committed over the years of that congregation's life. The church's prayer was augmented by preaching that called for personal conversion and renewal. A number of people came forward publicly declaring a new or renewed faith in Jesus as their Savior and Lord. Through prayer, new life began in that church.

"Truing" Ourselves

Using a vivid image from the construction industry, renowned scholar John C. Haughey, S.J., describes how a church is renewed (Haughey 2000). In construction, "to true" something is to build it according to specific and required specifications. The Holy Spirit, therefore, is the one who "trues" Christians, that is, forms them into the image and likeness of Jesus. In addition, it is the Holy Spirit who "trues" the community, the church, so that together they can become "a temple sacred in the Lord;...a dwelling place of God in the Spirit" (Eph. 2:21 NAB).

Among many instances in which God has given precise building instructions to his people is the account of Noah, who had the daunting task of constructing a huge ship while surrounded by people who ridiculed and criticized his efforts. To accomplish this task, God gave Noah specific directions and dimensions for the ark with which God would save his people (Gen. 6:14–16). By following God's directions, Noah became an effective instrument of God's power. Yet another example is seen in Exodus, where Moses receives specific directions and dimensions for building the sanctuary. In fact, God reminds Moses to make everything "according to the pattern shown you on the mountain" (Exod. 25:40), that is, the pattern of the sanctuary and its furnishings revealed to Moses on Mt. Sinai.

Just as God gave specific directions to Noah and had a specific plan for Moses, so the Lord has specific plans and directions for us as believers and for our churches. The plan or "pattern" for us, of course, is the pattern Jesus embodied throughout his life—the pattern that reached its clearest manifestation and expression on Calvary, where he revealed the transforming power of the cross.

Church leaders are called to work with God's Spirit by learning how "to true" according to the life and teachings of Christ and allowing themselves "to be trued" by the same. This process occurs through prayer (Haughey 2000).

In addition to learning how to encourage ways to fulfill people's need for competence, relatedness, and autonomy as described in the preceding chapters, a major part of church leaders' work is prayer. We are called to pray for our church on a regular basis, pleading with God to bless our members by bringing them to the fullness of life in Christ as the Lord adds to our number those who are being saved (see Acts 2:47).

Prayer: God's Way

We are all familiar with different approaches to prayer. There's the "911 Prayer": "Help! Get me out of here, God!" And the "Cleanup Prayer": "Lord, help straighten out this mess I'm in." Or the "Wish List Prayer": "These are the twelve things this church needs, Lord." Mercifully, our Heavenly Father hears all our prayers. Best, of course, is to pray as Jesus did, that *God's* will be done, not ours.

Making certain we are walking along God's path, then, becomes our first priority. Seeking his will at the start of each day, checking regularly with him throughout the day, and signing off at the day's end are the bare essentials for any Christian's walk. Leaders, however, are called to more. "I have so much to do today, I just don't have time to pray" becomes, as a Christian matures, "I have so much to do today, I must stop and pray."

Most readers, we trust, already recognize the correlation between the vitality of a person's prayer life and the joy experienced in ministry. Be confident, therefore, as you set out to do something new in your church. Ask, as did the earliest disciples, for the blessing of the Spirit. Be encouraged by Peter—a rather gruff fisherman, not a seminary-trained homilist—who preached to a crowd and saw thousands respond (Acts 2:14ff.). The Lord will be faithful, of this you can be certain.

The "God's ACRE" Program

We offer a prerequisite for any twenty-first century organizational initiative, an acronym: the God's ACRE Program. An acre represents the approximate footprint of most church buildings and immediate property, although we are very mindful of the many great houses of worship in this country that have only a room in a house or store front in which to hold services. As you set out, we hope this serves as a ready reminder:

A   *Autonomy:* acting with a sense of choice, participating volitionally

C   *Competence:* experiencing growth and optimal challenge to our current knowledge and ability

R   *Relatedness:* caring for others and being cared for in return

E   *Environment:* providing an atmosphere in which the above needs can be met,

> *which is all any leader can do,*
> *while praying without ceasing.*

Appendix 1

Ministry Position Description

Committee or Ministry: Mommy & Me.

Position: Facilitator.

Purpose of Position: To provide adult supervision and direction for facilitating the Mommy & Me group.

Responsibilities:

- Work with young children, fostering a Christian outlook through the day's lesson.
- Prepare and execute the day's lesson, keeping a Christian focus on the lesson's activity.
- Include parental participation whenever possible.

Qualifications:

- Completion of the diocesan volunteer reference registration process.
- Ability to work with children by relating to them in an affirming manner so that the day's lesson is communicated at the proper age level.
- Ability to invite and involve parents into the process in the hope of empowering them to work more effectively with their children at home in communicating the Christian faith.

See Trumbauer 1995 for further examples of descriptions of ministry positions.

- The energy and enthusiasm to work with groups of children during the weekly session.

Amount of Time Required: Two hours per week plus preparation time at home.

When Ministry Is Performed: Thursdays, 9:30–11:30 A.M.

Length of Commitment: One year.

On-Site Training Provided by: Ministry coordinators.

Responsible to: Ministry coordinators.

Support Provided by: Ministry coordinators, as well as the parish's Family Faith Coordinator.

Benefits:

- The joy of seeing children's lives enriched as they discover the faith in their ordinary experiences of play.
- The knowledge that your activity with parents and children has helped to foster a deeper faith expression for both.

Appendix 2

Letter of Call

What It Involves

In writing a letter of call, the following format seems to work best. Personalize the letter as much as you can. Clearly state the ministry you are asking the person to consider and the length of time involved. Identify the talents and gifts you have recognized that will help the individual serve effectively in the ministry. Indicate the areas of growth the person can anticipate while serving in the ministry. Finally, encourage the person to prayerfully consider the request, while referring to the Ministry Position Description (see appendix 1) for additional details. Indicate when you or another church leader will be in contact to receive the person's decision.

Sample

Date

Name
Address
City, State, Zip

Dear Firstname:

I invite you to consider prayerfully the call to serve as a member of Ministry of Hope, our church's ministry to the grieving. Your time of service would be for one year, renewable each year for an additional time of service.

I am inviting you to serve in this position because of your strong sense of the church's mission and your cheerful way of dealing with people. These gifts would enable you to offer a listening ear and a compassionate presence when helping a family prepare the funeral liturgy, serving on the team that visits the funeral home for a wake service, or accompanying a family as they attend the mass of Christian burial.

In addition, I believe this position will afford you the opportunity and satisfaction of growing stronger in the Lord as you serve in the sensitive area of helping others give back to God someone they love. It will strengthen your own faith and allow you the ongoing opportunity of seeing God work through the grieving process. As you know from your conversation with others on the team, all those who serve in the Ministry of Hope have found that they have received far more than have been asked to give.

I have enclosed a ministry description outlining the responsibilities and commitments involved. As you can see, there are three possible areas of service: working with the family in preparing the mass of Christian burial, participating in the wake prayer service, and assisting at the funeral mass on the day of burial. I believe that you would do well in any or all of these activities. Your participation would, of course, depend upon your personal schedule.

Since acceptance represents an investment of your time and giftedness, I know you will want to give this invitation some serious thought and prayer. For that reason I have asked one of our team members, _____, to call you next week to discuss any questions you may have. It is my hope that you will be able to say yes to this invitation to serve the parish in this important area of ministry.

Sincerely,
Name
Pastor

Appendix 3

Performance Appraisal Guidelines

1. Intend to enable the employee to grow further.
2. Presume the subordinate wants feedback ("How am I doing?").
3. Assume this adult is able to handle negative feedback (do not fuse).
4. Act emphatically (be sensitive to "learning moments").
5. Resist the "comma, but" syndrome; let positive and negative observations coexist.
6. Avoid using controlling language, for example, "I'm glad you listened to me when I suggested...."
7. Focus on behaviors, not character.
8. Treat any deficiencies as a business problem to be solved.
9. Do not promote competition within by drawing comparisons with a colleague.
10. Try to hear the subordinate's perspective.
11. Do not negotiate "ratings," but do correct any errors you realize you have made.
12. Anticipate growth; have a plan come out of the meeting.

13. Allow for a response, if the subordinate, upon reflection, has any questions or comments.
14. Use assertive, not aggressive speech, for example, "I believe you would benefit from..." and "What led you to...?"
15. Do not penalize new hires; use "N.A." or "Too soon to assess" rather than a deficient designation for someone too new to the function to be effective.

Appendix 4

Church Motivation Assessment Tool

Instructions for the Use of the Motivation Self-Assessment Questionnaire

When you conduct research with the public, including your church's membership, a number of issues are worth your careful attention. Foremost is the matter of confidentiality. If you suggest that respondents will be kept anonymous, privacy needs to be carefully assured. Using a third party is sometimes necessary; otherwise some demographic information offered by the respondent household might tip off the church leader conducting the survey, for example, "Age: 100+ years" might pinpoint the respondent's identity.

For this reason, we encourage you to involve an independent researcher, perhaps a friendly academic in your area. Such a person may be able to use his or her school stationery (purchased, and with permission to use, of course). This kind of arrangement allows the independent researcher to combine responses so that no respondent's evaluations are apparent. For example, the hundred-year-old can be combined with all those over eighty. Also, the use of an outside party can often bring additional credibility to a survey, especially if the person is from a respected academic institution. Ideally, the outside researcher can extend this courtesy on a *pro bono* basis (the academic author of this book welcomes questions from such volunteers at *baard@fordham.edu*).

Of course, if an independent researcher is not available, a

church or group of churches can still proceed. A task force, for example, can offer members the opportunity to fulfill the need for autonomy as they coordinate the task of distributing, collating, and analyzing the responses. The promise of confidentiality is a prerequisite for appointment to such a task force.

Comments on Church Research Methodology

Material

1. The Motivation Needs Index (MNI) and Christian Religious Internalization Scale (CRIS) scales, along with additional demographic data and relevant questions, appear on the two-page *Survey of Church Experience* below (see p. 134).*

2. The survey should be *printed on two sides of one sheet of a good quality stock,* that is, thicker than photocopy paper. Although this material is copyrighted, a properly formatted, reproducible, two-sided questionnaire, suitable for use in the field, is available without charge from Dr. Paul Baard at *baard@fordham.edu.*

3. An *annotated version* of the scales also appears at the end of this appendix for your scoring purposes (see p. 138). Note that all scores are add-ups (with negatively hyphenated scores reversed), to be used either in interchurch or before-and-after comparisons.

---

*The MNI is embedded in the first series of items labeled a–x. This scale assesses the satisfaction levels of the needs for competence, relatedness, and autonomy. On the bottom of the front of the survey form appears a series of demographic questions. On the back of the survey form will be found the CRIS scale, an assessment of the internalization of Christian values. This is an indicator of a person's intrinsic vs. extrinsic spiritual orientation. The bottom of this reverse side is available for any comments the survey respondent wishes to add.

4. A *sample cover letter* for prospective survey respondents also appears in this appendix (see p. 133). The reassurance of confidentiality is necessary since people are often reluctant to speak on the record in any negative way about their pastor or congregation. By assuring the congregation that their responses will not harm the pastor in any way you can expect greater cooperation and candor. If an independent researcher is not able to coordinate the survey, the special task force assigned to coordinate the project should sign the sample cover letter. In such cases, using the church's letterhead is acceptable.

Methodology

1. A *random sampling of members, drawn from a membership list,* increases the chances of wider representation than, for example, a street-interception approach focused on people leaving church. The problem with confining a sample to those present when the survey is taken is that those not present that particular week may be those who rarely attend and may well represent a significant proportion of the member list. In effect, they have already "voted with their feet," but without their input you will be unable to pinpoint what is motivationally wrong.

2. An *encouragement from the pulpit and bulletin* helps communicate that the survey is legitimate and important. (You can control overresponse by regular attendees by examining separately in the data analysis those indicating frequent and infrequent attendance).

3. *On the basis of experience, it is reasonable to expect a response rate of about 40–50 percent.* While this is generally considered adequate in research circles, the inclusion of a "gesture of thanks" with the mailing, that is, $1 or $2, has been found to increase the response to

over 50 percent and to about 70 percent, respectively. (We are aware that this recommendation steps into the world of extrinsic motivation, but for many this exercise is not intrinsically rewarding and may be deemed amotivating—that is, of little or no relevance or interest—to the prospective respondent. This is particularly true of the infrequent attender, who is of great import to church leaders.)

4. The inclusion of a *stamped, self-addressed envelope*—ideally to be returned to an academic institution—is essential.

5. If you need to raise response levels, a *reminder postcard* sent a week or so after the survey—along with pulpit and bulletin announcements—encourages cooperation. (The postcard reminder, however, is not essential if your budget is limited.)

6. If this is a study of more than one church, for example, of a selection of churches in a region or diocese, the *return envelope should be coded* so that responses can be properly attributed to their respective churches, for example, "Prof. Thomas J. Smith, c/o (university)" could be Church 1; "Prof. Thomas Smith, c/o (university)" for Church 2; "Prof. Tom Smith, c/o (university)" for Church 3, etc.

Or, more simply, a dot in the upper left corner of the envelope could be used for Church 1, lower left for Church 2, and lower right for Church 3.

This coding technique, although visible on the envelope, still preserves the commitment to holding the individual respondent anonymous. If you have provided any other assurances concerning this study, it is imperative that they be observed in the reporting of the data.

Cover Letter to Prospective Survey Respondents

[University Letterhead]

Date

Dear Church Member:

You have been randomly chosen for inclusion in a survey of opinions about church. Attached is an anonymous and confidential questionnaire.

The purpose of this study is to better understand the conditions that enhance a person's enjoyment of church activities, including worship services—*whether that individual attends often or occasionally*. Rev. _____ of the denomination's [or church's] headquarters and your own pastor, _____, have endorsed this research and ask you please to cooperate in it.

The results will help pastors better understand what can be done to encourage greater participation and enjoyment by all.

In no way will the findings be allowed to hurt or embarrass any pastor or church. The data will be combined with other samples and will be used only to identify the factors that affect people's experiences at church. We ask only that you, as an adult member of your household, (1) *complete the enclosed anonymous two-page survey* and (2) *mail it back within three days, if at all possible.*

I have enclosed a stamped, addressed envelope. If you would like to have a copy of the results sent to you, just put your return address on the outside envelope.

The results will be meaningful *only* if people like yourself—*whether you are an active member or not, and whether you attend often or seldom*—complete this survey.

Thank you for considering this request.

                                      Sincerely yours,
                                      [Name of researcher]
                                      Title

P.S.: If you care to add any comments, please write them on the back of the survey form.

Survey of Church Experience
(Strictly Confidential and Anonymous)

The following are statements about experiences at church. Your answers will *not* be revealed to anyone and will be used for church planning purposes only. Your input is very important—*whether you attend church often or just occasionally.*

Based upon how you usually find things to be at your local church, please indicate whether you agree or disagree with these statements by *circling* the number that best represents your own feelings, choosing one number of the seven:

1	2	3	4	5	6	7
not at all true			*somewhat true*			*very true*

Please circle one number for each item:

1 2 3 4 5 6 7   a. My church is very open to suggestions from its members.

1 2 3 4 5 6 7   **b. I really like the people at my church.**

1 2 3 4 5 6 7   c. I often feel like a failure at church.

1 2 3 4 5 6 7   **d. I am encouraged about my spiritual growth by people who attend my church.**

1 2 3 4 5 6 7   e. I feel pressured at church.

1 2 3 4 5 6 7   **f. I get along with the people at my church.**

1 2 3 4 5 6 7   g. I pretty much keep to myself at church.

1 2 3 4 5 6 7   **h. I don't think the sermons or homilies I hear at my church are very stimulating.**

1 2 3 4 5 6 7   i. I feel like I am free to express my ideas and opinions at my church.

1 2 3 4 5 6 7	j. **I consider the people at church to be my friends.**
1 2 3 4 5 6 7	k. I enjoy the challenges and opportunities to contribute my church provides.
1 2 3 4 5 6 7	l. **I've been able to learn interesting new things at my church.**
1 2 3 4 5 6 7	m. My church has a lot of rules about how to conduct my life.
1 2 3 4 5 6 7	n. **Most Sundays I feel a sense of satisfaction from attending church.**
1 2 3 4 5 6 7	o. My feelings are taken into consideration at my church.
1 2 3 4 5 6 7	p. **I don't get much of a chance to contribute my talents at my church.**
1 2 3 4 5 6 7	q. People at my church care about me.
1 2 3 4 5 6 7	r. **There are not many people at church whom I am close to.**
1 2 3 4 5 6 7	s. I feel I can be pretty much myself at church.
1 2 3 4 5 6 7	t. **The people I see at church do not seem to like me very much.**
1 2 3 4 5 6 7	u. I often do not feel very able to live my life in keeping with my church's teachings.
1 2 3 4 5 6 7	v. **At my church I feel a sense of having to do what I am told.**
1 2 3 4 5 6 7	w. People at church are pretty friendly toward me.
1 2 3 4 5 6 7	x. **I have a personally meaningful relationship with God.**

Demographic data

The age and sex of the person who completed this survey:

Age _____ Sex _____

The approximate level of household contributions to this church:

_____ percent of total income

I typically attend church:

_____ times each month / year
(please insert number, and *circle month or year*).

Just a few more questions...

People have different reasons for participating in religious activities. Please indicate whether you agree or disagree with the following statements by circling the number that best represents your own feelings, using:

1	2	3	4	5	6	7
not at all true			**somewhat true**			**very true**

1 2 3 4 5 6 7   aa. Church services give me a special chance to get close to God and to feel God close to me.

1 2 3 4 5 6 7   bb. **I attend church because others would disapprove if I didn't.**

1 2 3 4 5 6 7   cc. When I pray, I do so because I enjoy it.

1 2 3 4 5 6 7   dd. **I share my faith because God is important to me and I'd like others to know him too.**

1 2 3 4 5 6 7   ee. When I turn to God it is because it is satisfying to do so.

1 2 3 4 5 6 7   ff. **I attend church because one is supposed to.**

1 2 3 4 5 6 7   gg. I pray because God will disapprove if I don't.

1 2 3 4 5 6 7   hh. **I share my faith because I want other Christians to approve of me.**

1 2 3 4 5 6 7   ii. When I turn to God, it is because I enjoy spending time with Him.

1 2 3 4 5 6 7   jj. **I attend church because by going I learn new things.**

1 2 3 4 5 6 7   kk. When I pray, I do so because I find it satisfying.

1 2 3 4 5 6 7   ll. **I actively share my faith because I'd feel bad about myself if I didn't.**

1 2 3 4 5 6 7 mm. When I turn to God it is because I'd feel guilty if I didn't.

1 2 3 4 5 6 7   nn. **The single, most important reason why I attend church is to worship God.**

Thank you very much for your assistance.

Response Key for Survey of Church Experience

Scores are add-ups for each subscale: competence (COM), relatedness (REL), and autonomy (AUT); "rev" means reverse score. To reverse a score, change one to seven, two to six, etc.

ANNOTATED RESPONSE KEY TO MOTIVATION NEEDS INDEX (MNI)

1	2	3	4	5	6	7
not at all true			*somewhat true*			*very true*

1 2 3 4 5 6 7   a. My church is very open to suggestions from its members. (AUT)

1 2 3 4 5 6 7   **b. I really like the people at my church. (REL)**

1 2 3 4 5 6 7   c. I often feel like a failure at church. (COM-rev)

1 2 3 4 5 6 7   **d. I am encouraged about my spiritual growth by people who attend my church. (COM)**

1 2 3 4 5 6 7   e. I feel pressured at church. (AUT-rev)

1 2 3 4 5 6 7   **f. I get along with the people at my church. (REL)**

1 2 3 4 5 6 7   g. I pretty much keep to myself at church. (REL-rev)

1 2 3 4 5 6 7   **h. I don't think the sermons or homilies I hear at my church are very stimulating. (COM-rev)**

1 2 3 4 5 6 7   i. I feel like I am free to express my ideas and opinions at my church. (AUT)

1 2 3 4 5 6 7   **j. I consider the people at church to be my friends. (REL)**

1 2 3 4 5 6 7   k. I enjoy the challenges and opportunities to contribute my church provides. (COM)

1 2 3 4 5 6 7   **l. I've been able to learn interesting new things at my church. (COM)**

1 2 3 4 5 6 7   m. My church has a lot of rules about how to conduct my life. (AUT-rev)

1 2 3 4 5 6 7   **n. Most Sundays I feel a sense of satisfaction from attending church. (COM)**

1 2 3 4 5 6 7   o. My feelings are taken into consideration at my church. (AUT)

1 2 3 4 5 6 7   **p. I don't get much of a chance to contribute my talents at my church. (COM-rev)**

1 2 3 4 5 6 7   q. People at my church care about me. (REL)

1 2 3 4 5 6 7   **r. There are not many people at church whom I am close to. (REL-rev)**

1 2 3 4 5 6 7   s. I feel I can be pretty much myself at church. (AUT)

1 2 3 4 5 6 7   **t. The people I see at church do not seem to like me very much. (REL-rev)**

1 2 3 4 5 6 7   u. I often do not feel very able to live my life in keeping with my church's teachings. (COM-rev)

1 2 3 4 5 6 7   **v. At my church I feel a sense of having to do what I am told. (AUT-rev)**

1 2 3 4 5 6 7   w. People at church are pretty friendly toward me. (REL)

SCORING FOR MOTIVATION NEEDS INDEX (MNI)

Autonomy:
a + (reverse score for e) + i + (rev m) + o + s + (rev v)
= **Total for Autonomy**

Competence:
(rev c) + d + (rev h) + k + l + n + (rev p) + (rev u)
= **Total for Competence**

Relatedness:
b + f + (rev g) + j + q + (rev r) + (rev t) + w
= **Total for Relatedness**

Total for Autonomy + Total for Competence + Total for Relatedness = Total MNI Score

Note: Item x is included for purposes other than MNI score.

SCORING FOR CHRISTIAN RELIGIOUS INTERNALIZATION SCALE (CRIS)

Identification = cc + ee + gg + ii + jj = **Identification Score**

Introjection = bb + ff + hh + ll + mm = **Introjection Score**

Note: Items aa and nn are included for purposes other than CRIS score.

References

Aridas, Chris. 1998. *The Catholic Funeral: The Church's Ministry of Hope*. New York: Crossroad.

Baard, Paul P. In press. "Intrinsic Need Satisfaction in Organizations: A Motivational Basis of Success in For-Profit and Not-for-Profit Settings." In *Handbook of Self-determination Research*. Ed. Edward L. Deci and Richard M. Ryan. Rochester, N.Y.: University of Rochester Press.

———. 1994a. "A Motivational Guide for Consulting with Not-for-Profit Organizations: A Study of Church Growth and Participation." *Consulting Psychology Journal* 46:19–31.

———. 1994b. "Psychological Fusion and Personal Conflict in Organizations." *IEEE Transactions on Professional Communication* 37, no. 1 (March): 14–17.

———. 1994c. Response to S. Wetlaufer's "The Team That Wasn't." *Harvard Business Review* (November–December): 22–38.

———. 1998. "Interpersonal Stress in the Organization: The Role of Psychological Fusion." In *Corporate Communications for Executives*. Ed. Michael B. Goodman. Albany, N.Y.: State University of New York Press.

Baard, Paul P., and Susan M. Neville. 1996. "The Intrinsically Motivated Nurse: Help and Hindrance from Evaluation Feedback Sessions." *Journal of Nursing Administration* (July/August): 19–26.

Baard, Paul P., Edward L. Deci, and Richard M. Ryan. 1999. "Intrinsic Need Satisfaction: A Motivational Basis of Performance and Well-being in Work Settings." Unpublished manuscript. New York: Fordham University.

Barna, George. 2000a. Barna Research Group. *http://barna.org*. July 7, 2000.

———. 2000b. Barna Research Group. *http://barna.org*. August 23, 2000.

———. 2000c. Barna Research Group. *http://barna.org*. November 22, 2000.

Blanchard, Kenneth H., and Spencer Johnson. 1982. *The One Minute Manager*. New York: William Morrow.

Brockner, Joel. 1992. "Managing the Effects of Layoffs on Survivors." *California Management Review* 34, no. 2:9–28.

Carrell, Lori. 2000. *The Great American Survey*. Wheaton, Ill.: Mainstay Church Resources.

Cavalletti, Sofia. 1983. *The Religious Potential of the Child*. Trans. Patricia M. Coulter and Julie M. Coulter. New York: Paulist.

Champlin, Joseph M. 1997. "What Moves Some Catholics to Give More?" *Church* 13, no. 4 (Winter): 25–29.

Cimino, Richard, and Don Lattin. 1998. *Shopping for Faith: American Religion in the New Millennium*. San Francisco: Jossey-Bass.

Deci, Edward L. 1971. "Effects of Externally Mediated Rewards on Intrinsic Motivation." *Journal of Personality and Social Psychology* 18:105–15.

———. 1995. *Why We Do What We Do*. New York: Penguin.

Deci, Edward L., and Richard M. Ryan. 1985. *Intrinsic Motivation and Self-Determination in Human Behavior*. New York: Plenum.

Gallup, George Jr., and Timothy Jones. 2000. *The Next American Spirituality: Finding God in the Twenty-first Century*. Colorado Springs: Cook Communications Ministries.

Greeley, Andrew. 1984. *How to Save the Catholic Church*. New York: Viking Penguin.

Gwynne, S. C. 1990. "The Right Stuff." *Time Magazine*, October 29, 74–84.

Hadaway, C. K., P. L. Marler, and M. Chaves. 1993. "What the Polls Don't Show: A Closer Look at U.S. Church Attendance." *American Sociological Review* 50:741–52.

Hamner, Clay W. 1974. "Reinforcement Theory and Contingency Management in Organizational Settings." In *Organizational Behavior and Management: A Contingency Approach*. Ed. H. L. Tosi and W. C. Hamner. Chicago: St. Clair.

Haughey, John C. 2000. "Toward a Pneumatology of Lay Ministry." *Chicago Studies* 39, no. 1 (Spring): 27–46.

Kerr, Michael E., and Murray Bowen. 1988. *Family Evaluation*. New York: W. W. Norton.

Kohn, Alfie. 1993. *Punished by Rewards*. Boston: Houghton Mifflin.

O'Toole, Jack. 1996. *Forming the Future: Lessons from the Saturn Corporation*. Cambridge, Mass.: Blackwell.

Paul VI, Pope. 1975. *On Evangelization in the Modern World* (Evangelii Nuntiandi). Washington, D.C.: United States Catholic Conference.

Ronsvalle, John L., and Sylvia Ronsvalle. 1998. *The State of Church Giving through 1996*. Champaign, Ill.: Empty Tomb, Inc.

Ryan, Richard M., and Edward L. Deci. 2000. "Self-Determination Theory and the Facilitation of Intrinsic Motivation, Social Development, and Well-being." *American Psychologist* 55, no. 1 (January): 68–78.

Trumbauer, Jean Morris. 1995. *Sharing the Ministry*. Minneapolis: Augsburg.

Warren, Rick. 1995. *The Purpose-Driven Church*. Grand Rapids, Mich.: Zondervan.

Weddell, Sherry Anne, and Michael Sweeney. 1998. *The Called and Gifted Workshop*. Audiotape workshop by Sherry Anne Weddell and Michael Sweeney. Seattle: Catherine of Siena Institute.